DATE DUE

NR 2 9 '99			
SE 2 3 '99			

DEMCO 38-296

CAREERS

in Focus

CONSTRUCTION

Ferguson Publishing Company
Chicago, Illinois

Copyright © 1998 Ferguson Publishing Company
ISBN 0-89434-218-5

Library of Congress Cataloging-in-Publication Data

Careers in focus.   Construction.
      p.   cm.
    Includes bibliographical references and index.
    Summary: Explores the top twenty-seven careers in construction
in terms of the nature of the work, educational or training requirements, getting started, advancement possibilities, salary, employment
outlook, and sources of more information.
    ISBN 0-89434-218-5
      1. Building trades--Vocational guidance--Juvenile literature. [1.
Building trades--Vocational guidance. 2. Vocational guidance.]
    TH159.C37   1997
    690'.023--dc21   97-22130
                                                         CIP
                                                          AC

Printed in the United States of America

Published and distributed by
Ferguson Publishing Company
200 West Madison Street, Suite 300
Chicago, Illinois 60606
312-580-5480

U-8

Table of Contents

Bricklayers and Stonemasons

School Subjects
Mathematics
Shop

Personal Interests
Building things
Fixing things

Work Environment
Indoors and outdoors
Primarily multiple locations

Minimum Education Level
High school diploma
Apprenticeship

Salary Range
$13,600 to $43,600

Certification or Licensing
None

Outlook
As fast as the average

DOT: 861   **GOE:** 05.05.01   **NOC:** 7281

Definition

Bricklayers are skilled workers who construct and repair walls, partitions, floors, arches, fireplaces, chimneys, and other structures from brick, concrete block, gypsum block, and pre-cast panels made of terra cotta, structural tile, and other masonry materials. *Stonemasons* build stone walls, floors, piers, and other structures, and they set the decorative stone exteriors of structures such as churches, hotels, and public buildings.

History

Sun-baked clay bricks were used in constructing buildings more than six thousand years ago in Mesopotamia. Along with brick, stone was used in ancient Egypt in many structures. The Romans introduced masonry construction to the rest of Europe and made innovations in bricklaying, including the use of mortar and different types of bonds, or patterns. As the Roman Empire declined, so did the art of bricklaying. During the period of cathedral building in Europe, from about the tenth century to the seventeenth century, stonemasons formed guilds in various cities and towns. These guilds functioned much as today's unions do. They had the same categories of workers: apprentices, journeymen, and masters. Not until the great fire of London in 1666 did the English start to use brick again in building. The Chinese also were expert in bricklaying and stonemasonry, the best example of their work being the Great Wall of China. High in the Andes of South America, Incan stoneworkers had perfected their art by the twelfth century.

Although some brick houses made with imported bricks were built in Florida by the Spaniards, the first bricks made by Europeans in North America were manufactured in Virginia in 1612. These bricks were handmade from clay, just as they were in ancient times. Machines were not used in the manufacturing of bricks until the mid-eighteenth century. Changes in the content of bricks came shortly afterwards. Concrete and cinder blocks were developed at this time, as was structural clay tile. The patent for a sand brick, which is a combination of sand and hydrated lime, was granted about this time, too.

Today, attractive kinds of brick, called face brick, can be used in places where appearance is especially important. The use of face brick has helped to popularize brick in modern construction. Various colors of brick can be made by using iron oxides, iron sulfides, and other materials. By varying the bond and the hue of brick, many interesting artistic effects can be achieved.

Stone is a very durable, adaptable material for building purposes, although one of its drawbacks is that it may be much more difficult to cut and to transport than alternative materials. Today it remains popular, particularly as a way to enhance the appearance of important structures such as hotels, public buildings, and churches. In modern construction, a thin covering of stone veneer about two inches thick is applied in various patterns to exterior surfaces of buildings. The veneer is anchored and supported on a steel frame.

Nature of the Work

When bricklayers or stonemasons begin work on a job, they usually start by examining a blueprint or drawing to determine the designer's specifications. Then they measure the work area to fix reference points and guidelines in accordance with the blueprint.

If they are building a wall, bricklayers traditionally start with the corners, or leads, which must be precisely established if the finished structure is to be sound and straight. The corners may be established by more experienced bricklayers, with the task of filling in between the corners left to less experienced workers. Corner posts, or masonry guides, may be used to define the line of the wall, speeding the building process. A first, dry course may be put down without mortar so that the alignment and positioning of the brick can be checked.

In laying brick, bricklayers use a metal trowel to spread a bed or layer of soft mortar on a prepared base. Then they set the brick into the mortar, tapping and working each brick into the correct position. Excess mortar is cut off, and the mortar joints are smoothed with special tools that give a neat, uniform look to the wall. In walls, each layer, or course, is set so that vertical joints do not line up one on top of another, but instead form a pleasing, regular pattern. The work must be continually checked for horizontal and vertical straightness with mason's levels, gauge strips, plumb lines, and other equipment. Sometimes it is necessary to cut and fit brick to size using a power saw or hammer and chisel. Around doors and windows, bricklayers generally use extra steel supports in the wall.

Bricklayers must know how to mix mortar, which is made of cement, sand, and water, and how to spread it so that the joints throughout the structure will be evenly spaced, with a neat appearance. They may have helpers who mix the mortar as well as move materials and scaffolding around the work site as needed.

Some bricklayers specialize in working with one type of masonry material only, such as gypsum block, concrete block, hollow tile used in partitions, or terra-cotta products. Other bricklayers, called *refractory masons,* work in the steel and glass manufacturing industries and specialize in installing firebrick and refractory tile linings of furnaces, kilns, boilers, cupolas, and other high-temperature equipment. Still others are employed to construct manholes and catch basins in sewers.

Stonemasons work with two types of stone: natural cut stone, such as marble, granite, limestone, or sandstone; and artificial stone, which is made to order from concrete, marble chips, or other masonry materials. They set the stone in many kinds of structures, including piers, walls, walks, arches, floors, and curbstones. On some projects, the drawings that stonemasons work from specify where to set certain stones that have been previously identified by number. In such cases, helpers may locate the stones and bring them to the masons. Large stones may have to be hoisted into place with derricks.

In building stone walls, masons begin by setting a first course of stones in a bed of mortar, then build upward by alternating layers of mortar and stone courses. At every stage, they may use leveling devices and plumb lines, correcting the alignment of each stone. They often insert wedges and tap the stones into place with rubber mallets. Once a stone is in a good position, they remove the wedges, fill the gaps with mortar, and smooth the area using a metal tool called a tuck pointer. Large stones may need to be anchored in place with metal brackets that are welded or bolted to the wall.

Similarly, when masons construct stone floors, they begin by spreading mortar. They place stones, adjusting their positions using mallets and crowbars, and periodically checking the levelness of the surface. They may cut some stones into smaller pieces to fit, using hammer and chisel or a power saw with a diamond blade. After all the stones are placed, the masons fill the joints between the stones with mortar and wash off the surface.

Some stonemasons specialize in setting marble. Others work exclusively on setting alberene, which is an acid-resistant soapstone used in industrial settings on floors and for lining vats and tanks. Other specialized stone workers include *composition stone applicators, monument setters, patchers,* and *chimney repairers.* Stone repairers mend broken slabs made of marble and similar stone.

Bricklayers and stonemasons sometimes use power tools, such as saws and drills, but for the most part they use hand tools, including trowels, jointers, hammers, rulers, chisels, squares, gauge lines, mallets, brushes, and mason's levels.

Requirements

The best way to become a bricklayer or stonemason is to complete an apprenticeship. Vocational schools also provide training in these fields. However, many people learn their skills informally on the job simply by observing and helping experienced workers. The disadvantage of this approach is that informal training is likely to be less thorough, and it may take workers much longer to learn the full range of necessary skills for the trade.

Apprenticeship programs are sponsored by contractors or jointly by contractors and unions. Nonunion-sponsored programs also exist. Applicants for apprenticeships need to be at least seventeen years old and in good physical condition. High school graduates are usually preferred. A good background for applicants would include any available high school courses in shop, basic mathematics, blueprint reading, and mechanical drawing.

Apprentices spend three years learning as they work under the supervision of experienced bricklayers or stonemasons. In addition, they receive at least 144 hours of classroom instruction in related subjects such as blueprint reading, applied mathematics, and layout work. In the work portion of their apprenticeship, they begin with simple jobs, like carrying materials and building scaffolds. After they become familiar with one task, they change to another, eventually experiencing a broad range of activities. In the course of an apprenticeship, a worker can become qualified to work with more than one kind of masonry material.

Inexperienced beginners who plan to learn the trade informally and on the job usually begin as helpers or laborers doing simple tasks. They learn more complex jobs whenever the opportunity presents itself. As they gradually become more useful employees, they may find more ways to increase their skills.

Opportunities for Experience & Exploration

Opportunities are limited for most high school students to directly experience the work in the field of bricklaying and stonemasonry. Occasionally it is possible for students to secure summer employment on construction projects and observe bricklayers or stonemasons. Students who are already enrolled in vocational bricklaying programs can gain some practical experience as part of their instruction. Otherwise, a field trip to a construction site can give an overall view of the type of work done by bricklayers and stonemasons.

Methods of Entering

The two main ways that people start out in these fields are in formal apprenticeship programs and as helpers or laborers who gradually learn on the job. Helper jobs can be found through newspaper want ads, at the local office of the state employment service, or by contacting appropriate contractors.

People seeking to apply for apprenticeships can obtain more information from local contractors who hire bricklayers or stonemasons, the state employment service, or the local office of the International Union of Bricklayers and Allied Craftsmen. The Mason Contractors Association of America can also be of help.

Another option may be to enter a bricklaying program at a vocational school. Such a program combines classroom instruction with work experience. Vocational school placement offices may be able to help qualified graduates secure jobs that use their skills.

Advancement

Bricklayers and stonemasons with enough skill and experience may advance to supervisory positions. Some union contracts require a supervisor if three or more workers are employed on a job.

Supervisors sometimes become superintendents at large construction sites. With additional technical training, bricklayers and stonemasons may become cost estimators. Cost estimators look at building plans, obtain quotations on masonry material, and prepare and submit bids on the costs of doing the proposed job. Another possible advancement is to become a city or county inspector who checks to see if the work done by contractors meets local building code regulations. A few bricklayers and stonemasons go into business for themselves as contractors.

Employment Outlook

There are about 190,000 bricklayers and stonemasons employed in the United States. Over the next ten to fifteen years, employment opportunities in both fields are expected to rise at rates about the same as the average for all other occupations. There will probably be increased construction of many kinds of buildings, and the popularity of brick and stone is growing, especially ornamental brickwork and stonework on building fronts and in lobbies. However, technological developments in construction techniques will affect the job outlook. For example, bricklayers will probably be installing more precast panels made of various types of masonry material instead of individual bricks, a trend that may tend to restrain the demand for bricklayers. Bricklayers who specialize in refractory repair will also find their job opportunities declining.

During economic downturns, bricklayers and stonemasons, like other workers in construction-related jobs, can expect to have fewer job opportunities and perhaps be laid off.

Earnings

The median annual earnings of bricklayers and stonemasons are over $26,000, with a range between about $13,600 and $43,600. Most make between $17,400 and $35,600. Earnings for those who work outside can be affected by bad weather, and earnings are lower for workers in areas where the local economy is in a slump. The pay also varies according to geographical region, with rates highest in the West.

The beginning hourly rate for apprentices is about half of the rate for experienced workers. In addition to regular pay, various fringe benefits such as health and life insurance, pensions, and paid vacations are available to many workers in this field.

Conditions of Work

Most bricklayers and stonemasons have a forty-hour workweek. They are usually paid time-and-a-half for overtime and double-time for work on Saturdays, Sundays, and holidays.

Most of the work is done outdoors, where conditions may be dusty, hot, cold, or damp. Often workers must stand on scaffolds that are high off the ground. They may need to bend or stoop constantly to pick up materials. They may be on their feet most of the working day, or they may kneel for long periods.

Some of the hazards in this work are falling off a scaffold, being hit by falling material, and other injuries common to lifting and handling heavy material. But whereas poor weather conditions used to affect work schedules and job site conditions, protective sheeting is now used to enclose work areas. This sheeting makes it possible to work through most inclement weather.

Apprentices and experienced workers must furnish their own hand tools and measuring devices. Contractors supply the materials for making mortar, scaffolding, lifts, ladders, and other large equipment used in the construction process.

Well-qualified bricklayers and stonemasons can often find work at wages higher than those of most other construction workers. But because the work is seasonal, bricklayers and stonemasons must plan carefully to make it through any periods of unemployment.

Sources of Additional Information

Associated General Contractors of America
1957 E Street, NW
Washington, DC 20006
Tel: 202-393-2040
Email: 73264.15@compuserv.com
WWW: http://agc.org

Brick Institute of America
11490 Commerce Park Drive
Reston, VA 22091
Tel: 703-620-0010

Bricklayers and Stonemasons

■ **Clay Brick Association of Canada**
#GZ, 1 Sparks Avenue
Willowdale, ON M2H 2W1 Canada
Tel: 416-695-8388

■ **International Union of Bricklayers and Allied Craftsmen**
815 15th Street, NW
Washington, DC 20005
Tel: 202-783-3788

■ **National Association of Home Builders**
Home Builders Institute
15th and M Streets, NW
Washington, DC 20005
Tel: 202-822-0200
Email: 75300.52@compuserv.com
WWW: http://www.nahb.com

Carpenters

School Subjects
  Mathematics
  Shop

Personal Interests
  Building things
  Fixing things

Work Environment
  Indoors and outdoors
  Primarily multiple locations

Minimum Education Level
  High school diploma
  Apprenticeship

Salary Range
  $12,400 to $50,000

Certification or Licensing
  None

Outlook
  About as fast as the average

DOT: 860   **GOE:** 05.05.02   **NOC:** 7271

Definition

Carpenters cut, shape, level, and fasten together pieces of wood and other construction materials, such as wallboard, plywood, and insulation. Many carpenters work on constructing, remodeling, or repairing houses and other kinds of buildings. Other carpenters work at construction sites where roads, bridges, docks, boats, mining tunnels, and wooden vats are built. A carpenter may specialize in building the rough framing of a structure, and thus be considered a *rough carpenter,* or he or she may specialize in the finishing details of a structure, such as the trim around doors and windows, and thus be considered a *finish carpenter.*

History

Wood has been used as a building material since the dawn of civilization. Tools that resembled modern hand tools first began to be made around 1500 BC, By the Middle Ages, many of the basic techniques and the essential tools of carpentry were perfected, and they have changed little since that time.

However, the role of carpenters has changed. In the past, buildings were mostly built with braced-frame construction, which made use of large, heavy timbers held together with mortised joints and diagonal bracing. In this kind of construction, carpenters were often the principal workers on a house or other building. Since the mid-nineteenth century, balloon-frame construction, which makes use of smaller and lighter pieces of wood, has simplified the construction process, and concrete and steel have replaced wood for many purposes, especially in floors and roofs. But as some carpentry tasks in building construction have become easier, other new jobs, such as making forms for poured concrete, have added to the importance of carpenters at construction sites.

Nature of the Work

Carpenters are the largest group of workers in the building trades. There are over a million carpenters in the United States today. About 80 percent of them work for contractors involved in building, repairing, and remodeling buildings and other structures. Manufacturing firms, schools, stores, and government bodies employ most other carpenters.

Carpenters do two basic kinds of work: rough carpentry and finish carpentry. Rough carpenters construct and install temporary structures and supports, wooden structures used in industrial settings, as well as parts of buildings that are usually covered up when the rooms are finished. Among the structures built by such carpenters are scaffolds for other workers to stand on, chutes used as channels for wet concrete, forms for concrete foundations, and timber structures that support machinery. In buildings, they may put up the frame and install rafters, joists, subflooring, wall sheathing, prefabricated wall panels and windows, and many other components.

Finish carpenters install hardwood flooring, staircases, shelves, cabinets, trim on windows and doors, and other woodwork and hardware that make the building look complete, inside and outside. Finish carpentry requires especially careful, precise workmanship, because the result must have a good appearance, in addition to being sturdy. Many carpenters who are employed by building contractors do both rough and finish work on buildings.

Although they do many different tasks in different settings, carpenters generally follow approximately the same basic steps. First they look over blueprints or plans for information (or get instructions from a supervisor) about the dimensions of the structure to be built and the type of materials to be used. Sometimes local building codes determine how a structure should be built, so carpenters need to know about such regulations. Using rulers, framing squares, chalk lines, and other measuring and marking equipment, they lay out how the work will be done. Using hand and power tools, they cut and shape the wood, plywood, fiberglass, plastic, or other materials. Then they nail, screw, glue, or staple the pieces together. Finally, they use levels, plumb bobs, rulers, and squares to check their work, and they make any necessary adjustments. Sometimes carpenters work with prefabricated units for components such as wall panels or stairs. Installing these is, in many ways, a much less complicated task, because much less layout, cutting, and assembly work is needed.

Carpenters who work outside of the building construction field may do a variety of installation and maintenance jobs, such as repairing furniture, changing locks, and installing ceiling tiles or exterior siding on buildings. Other carpenters specialize in building, repairing, or modifying ships, wooden boats, wooden railroad trestles, timber framing in mine shafts, woodwork inside railcars, storage tanks and vats, or stage sets in theaters.

Requirements

Carpenters can acquire the skills of their trade in various ways, through formal training programs and through informal on-the-job training. Of the different ways to learn, an apprenticeship is considered the best, because it provides a more thorough and complete foundation for a career as a carpenter than other kinds of training. However, the limited number of available apprenticeships means that not all carpenters can learn their trade this way.

Many carpenters pick up skills informally on the job while they work as carpenter's helpers. Usually employers prefer applicants who have completed high school. They begin with little or no training and gradually learn as they work under the supervision of experienced carpenters. The skills that helpers develop depend on the jobs that their employers contract to do. Working for a small contracting company, a beginner may learn about relatively few kinds of carpentry tasks. On the other hand, a large contracting company may offer a wider variety of opportunities to learn. Becoming a skilled carpenter by this method can take much longer than an apprenticeship, and the completeness of the training varies. Some people who are waiting for an apprenticeship to become available work as helpers to gain experience in the field.

Some people first learn about carpentry while serving in the U.S. armed forces. Other carpenters learn skills in vocational educational programs offered in trade schools and in correspondence courses. Vocational programs can be very good, especially as a supplement to other practical training. But without additional hands-on instruction, vocational school graduates may not be well enough prepared to get many jobs in the field, because some programs do not provide sufficient opportunity for students to practice and perfect their carpentry skills.

Apprenticeships usually last three to four years. They are administered by employer groups and local chapters of various labor unions that organize carpenters. Applicants for apprenticeships must meet the specific requirements of local apprenticeship committees. Typically, applicants must be at least seventeen years old and must show that they have some aptitude for carpentry and enough education to complete the training.

Apprenticeships combine on-the-job work experience with classroom instruction in a planned, systematic program. Initially, apprentices work at such simple tasks as building concrete forms, doing rough framing, and nailing subflooring. Toward the end of their training apprentices may work on finishing trimwork, fitting hardware, hanging doors, and building stairs. In the course of this experience, they become familiar with the tools, materials, techniques, and equipment of the trade, and they learn how to do layout, framing, finishing, and other basic carpentry jobs.

The work experience is supplemented by about 144 hours of classroom instruction per year. Some of this instruction concerns the correct use and maintenance of tools, safety practices, first aid, building code requirements, and the properties of different construction materials. Among other subjects that apprentices study are the principles of layout, blueprint reading, shop mathematics, and sketching. Both on the job and in the classroom, carpenters learn how to work effectively with members of other skilled building trades.

A good high school background for prospective carpenters would include carpentry and woodworking courses, as well as other shop classes, applied mathematics, mechanical drawing, and blueprint reading. Carpenters need to have manual dexterity, good eye-hand coordination, and a good sense of balance. They need to be in good physical condition, because the work involves a great deal of activity. Stamina is much more important than physical strength. On the job, carpenters may have to climb, stoop, kneel, crouch, and reach.

Opportunities for Experience & Exploration

High school students may begin finding out about the work that carpenters do by taking courses such as wood shop, applied mathematics, drafting, and other industrial arts. Simple projects such as building birdhouses or shelving at home can also help people gauge their ability and interest in the field. In addition, summer employment at a construction site can provide students with a useful overview of the work performed in the construction industry and perhaps the opportunity to talk with carpenters on the job.

Methods of Entering

Two important ways of starting out in carpentry are participating in an apprenticeship program and gradually gaining experience and skills on the job. Information about apprenticeships can be obtained by contacting the local office of the state employment service, area contractors that hire carpenters, or the local offices of the United Brotherhood of Carpenters and Joiners of America, a union that cooperates in sponsoring apprenticeships. Helper jobs that can be filled by beginners without special training in carpentry may be advertised in newspaper classified ads or with the state employment service. Another possibility is contacting potential employers directly.

Advancement

After they have completed and met all the requirements of their apprenticeship training, former apprentices are considered journeymen carpenters. After they have gained enough experience, journeymen carpenters may be promoted to positions where they are responsible for supervising the work of other carpenters. If their background includes exposure to a broad range of construction activities, they may eventually advance to positions as general construction supervisors. Carpenters who are skillful at mathematical computations and have a good knowledge of the construction business may become estimators. Some carpenters go into business for themselves, doing repair or construction work as independent contractors.

Employment Outlook

Overall, the outlook for carpenters over the next ten to fifteen years is about the same as the average for other occupational fields. Total employment of carpenters is expected to increase moderately, as new construction and renovations of existing structures continue. But at any one time, building activity and thus job opportunities will be better in some geographic areas than in others, reflecting regional and local variations in economic conditions.

Even if construction activity is strong in coming years, several factors will contribute to a slower rate of employment growth than at times in the past. One factor affecting growth is the trend toward increasing the use of prefabricated building components, which are more quickly and easily installed than parts made by traditional construction methods. The use of prefabricated materials is likely to mean that fewer skilled carpenters will be needed. In addition, many new lightweight, cordless tools like nailers and drills are making the work of carpenters easier and faster, and thus tending to reduce the total number of workers needed.

Job turnover is relatively high in the carpentry field. Many people prefer to switch to another occupation after working for awhile because they find their skills are too limited to get the best jobs or they don't like the work. As a result, every year thousands of job openings will become available. Carpenters with good all-around skills, such as those who have completed apprenticeships, will have the best chances of being hired for the most desirable positions.

Nonetheless, carpenters can expect that they may go through periods of unemployment. The number of available jobs is always related to various economic factors, and during an economic downturn, fewer building projects are started. Carpenters need to plan for the possibility of major ups and downs in their income.

Earnings

In the 1990s, the majority of carpenters who do not own their own businesses have earnings that range between $15,800 and $29,700 per year. Some make as little as about $12,400, while a few have earnings between $40,000 and $50,000.

Starting pay for apprentices is about 50 percent of the experienced worker's pay scale. It is increased periodically so that by the last phase of training the pay of apprentices is 85 to 90 percent of the journeyman carpenter's rate. Fringe benefits, such as health insurance, pension funds, and paid vacations, are available to most workers in this field and vary with local union contracts.

Conditions of Work

Carpenters may work either indoors or outdoors. If they are engaged in rough carpentry, they probably do most of their work outdoors. They may have to work on high scaffolding or in a basement making cement forms. A construction site can be noisy, dusty, hot, cold, or muddy. Often carpenters must be physically active throughout the day, constantly standing, stooping, climbing, and reaching. Some of the possible hazards of the job include being hit by falling objects, falling off a ladder, straining muscles, and getting cuts and scrapes on fingers and hands. Carpenters who follow recommended safety practices and procedures can minimize these hazards.

Work in the construction industry involves changing from one job location to another, and from time to time being laid off because of poor weather, shortages of materials, or simply lack of jobs. Workers in this field must thus be able to arrange their finances so that they can make it through sometimes long periods of unemployment. Most carpenters belong to the United Brotherhood of Carpenters and Joiners of America.

Sources of Additional Information

■ **Associated General Contractors of America**
1957 E Street, NW
Washington, DC 20006
Tel: 202-393-2040

■ **National Association of Home Builders**
15th and M Streets, NW
Washington, DC 20005
Tel: 202-822-0200

■ **Ontario Carpentry Contractors Association**
#305, 1 Greensboro Drive
Rexdale, ON M9W 1C8 Canada
Tel: 416-248-6213

■ **United Brotherhood of Carpenters and Joiners of America**
101 Constitution Avenue, NW
Washington, DC 20001
Tel: 202-546-6206

Cement Masons

School Subjects
Mathematics
Shop

Personal Interests
Building things
Drawing/painting

Work Environment
Primarily outdoors
Primarily multiple locations

Minimum Education Level
High school diploma
Apprenticeship

Salary Range
$13,100 to $40,000+

Certification or Licensing
None

Outlook
Little change or more slowly than average

DOT: 844   **GOE:** 05.05.01   **NOC:** 7282

Definition

Cement masons are skilled workers who place and finish the concrete surfaces in many different kinds of construction projects ranging from small patios and sidewalks to highways, dams, and airport runways.

History

Cement is a building material that hardens when mixed with water. Various kinds of cement have been used for thousands of years. The ancient Egyptians and the Greeks both made cements, but the most effective cements were made by the Romans. They developed a kind of cement made from slaked lime and volcanic ash and used it throughout Europe in building of roads, aqueducts, bridges, and other structures. After the collapse of the Roman Empire, the art of making cement mostly disappeared.

In the eighteenth century, through the experiments of an English engineer, John Smeaton, a cement was developed that set up even under water. Smeaton successfully used this cement in building the famous Eddystone Lighthouse, in Devon, England. Later it was used in some parts of the Erie Canal, the waterway built to connect the Great Lakes and New York City.

In 1824, an English stonemason, Joseph Aspdin, developed the first portland cement mixture. To make it, he burned and ground together limestone and clay. He called his product "portland" cement because it resembled the limestone quarried on the Isle of Portland. Portland cement was very strong and water-resistant, and it soon became the most widely used cement. The first American portland cement plant was built in 1871. Cement manufactured today is essentially the same material as Aspdin's portland cement.

Cement is seldom used by itself in large quantities. More often, it is mixed with another material. Cement mixed with sand forms mortar that is used, for example, in brick walls and buildings. Cement mixed with gravel or crushed rock forms concrete, which is a cheap, versatile, strong, and durable structural material. Today concrete is one of the most widely used building materials in the world. With the development of ways to reinforce concrete with metal and the appropriate machinery for handling it, concrete has become useful for many purposes, including bridges, roofs, highways, dams, swimming pools, sculpture, fence posts, helicopter pads, and missile launching sites.

Nature of the Work

The principal work of cement masons, also known as *concrete masons,* is to put into place and then smooth and finish concrete surfaces in a variety of different construction projects. Sometimes they add colors to the concrete to change its appearance or chemicals to speed up or slow down the time that the concrete takes to harden. They use various tools to create specified surface textures on fresh concrete before it sets. They may also fabricate beams, columns, or panels of concrete. Most cement masons are employed by concrete contractors or general contractors to help build roads, shopping malls, factories, and many other structures. A small number of masons are employed by manufacturers of concrete products.

Cement masons must know their materials well. They must be able to judge how long different concrete mixtures will take to set up and how factors like heat, cold, and wind will affect the curing, or hardening, of the cement. They need to be able to recognize these effects by examining and touching the concrete. They need to know about the strengths of different kinds of concrete and how different surface appearances are produced.

In addition to understanding the materials they work with, cement masons must also be familiar with blueprint reading, applied mathematics, building code regulations, and the procedures involved in estimating costs and quantities of materials.

On a construction job, the preparation of the site where the concrete will be poured is very important. Cement masons begin by setting up the forms that will hold the wet concrete until it hardens into the desired shape. The forms must be properly aligned and must allow for concrete of the correct dimensions, as specified in the original design. In some structures, reinforcing steel rods or mesh are set into place after the forms are put in position. The cement masons then pour or direct the pouring of the concrete into the forms so that it flows smoothly rather than drops unevenly. The cement masons or their helpers spread and tamp the fresh concrete into place. Then the masons level the surface by moving a straightedge back and forth across the top of the forms.

Using a bull float, which is a large wooden trowel, cement masons begin the smoothing operation. This process covers up the larger particles in the wet concrete and brings to the surface the fine cement paste in the mixture. On projects where curved edges are desired, cement masons may use an edger or a radius tool, guiding it around the edge between the form and the concrete. They may make grooves or joints at intervals in the surface to help control cracking.

The process continues with more finishing work, either done by hand with a small metal trowel or with a power trowel. This smoothing gets out most remaining irregularities on the surface. On driveways, sidewalks, and similar projects, cement masons may use a brush or broom on the concrete to attain a nonslip surface texture. Or they may embed pebbles in the surface. Afterward, the concrete must cure to reach its proper strength, a process that can take about a week.

On structures like walls or columns that expose surfaces when the forms are removed, cement masons must leave a smooth and uniform finish. To achieve this, they may rub down high spots with an abrasive material, chip out rough or defective spots with a chisel and hammer, and fill low areas with cement paste. They may finish off the exposed surface with a coating of a cement mixture to create an even, pleasing appearance.

Cement masons use a variety of hand and power tools, ranging from simple chisels, hammers, trowels, edgers, and leveling devices to pneumatic chisels, concrete mixers, and troweling machines. Smaller projects like sidewalks and patios may be done by hand. But on large-scale projects like highways, power-operated floats and finishing equipment are necessary. Although power equipment can speed many tasks, on most projects there are still corners or other inaccessible areas that require hand work.

There are various specialists whose jobs involve covering, leveling, and smoothing cement and concrete surfaces. Among them are *concrete-stone finishers,* who work with ornamental stone and concrete surfaces; *concrete rubbers,* who polish concrete surfaces; and *nozzle cement sprayers,* who use spray equipment to apply cement mixtures to surfaces.

Poured concrete wall technicians are another occupational group whose activities are related to those of cement masons. These workers use surveying instruments to mark construction sites for excavation and to set up and true (that is, align correctly) concrete forms. They direct the pouring of concrete to form walls of buildings, and, after removing the forms, they may waterproof lower walls and lay drainage tile to promote drainage away from the building. Unlike cement masons, however, poured concrete technicians generally have at least two years of technical training in such subjects as surveying and construction methods.

Requirements

Cement masons can learn their skills either on the job or in apprenticeship programs. Many people with no special skills or experience begin work in helper positions and gradually learn the trade informally over an uncertain number of years by working with experienced masons. However, apprenticeships are the recommended way to acquire the necessary skills, because they provide more balanced, in-depth training through programs that last two to three years.

Many cement masons who pick up skills on the job begin as construction laborers or cement mason helpers. In considering applicants for helper jobs, most employers prefer to hire people who are at least eighteen, who are in good physical condition, and who possess a driver's license. The ability to get along with coworkers is important, because cement masons often work in teams. Although a high school diploma may not be required, applicants who have taken high school shop courses, blueprint reading, and mechanical drawing may have an advantage. Trainees usually begin with easy tasks such as edging and jointing, then progress to more difficult work such as final finishing of surfaces.

Apprenticeships are usually jointly sponsored by local contractors and unions. Applicants for apprenticeship programs sometimes must be approved by the local joint labor–management apprenticeship committee. They may have to take a written test and pass a physical examination. The training consists of a combination of planned work experience and classroom instruction. On the job, apprentices learn about handling the tools and materials of the trade, about layout work and finishing techniques, and about job safety. The classroom instruction involves at least 144 hours each year in such related subjects as mathematics, blueprint reading, architectural drawing, procedures for estimating materials and costs, and local building regulations.

Opportunities for Experience & Exploration

High school students can learn more about their own aptitude for this kind of work by taking courses such as general mathematics, drafting, and various shop classes. In addition, summer employment as part of a construction crew can provide valuable firsthand experience. Some people are introduced to the building construction trades, including the work of cement masons, while they are serving in the military, especially with the Army Engineering Corps.

Methods of Entering

People who want to become cement masons can enter this field either through formal apprenticeship training programs or by obtaining a job that offers the opportunity for on-the-job training. For information about becoming an apprentice cement mason, it is possible to contact local cement contractors, the offices of the state employment service, or the area headquarters of one of the unions that organize cement masons. Many cement masons are members of either the Operative Plasterers and Cement Masons International Association of the United States of America or the International Union of Bricklayers and Allied Craftsmen.

People who wish to become on-the-job trainees can contact directly contractors in the area who may be hiring helpers. They may also want to follow up on job leads from the state employment service or newspaper classified ads.

Advancement

After they have gained some skills and become efficient workers in their trade, cement masons may specialize in one phase of the work. They may become, for example, *lip-curb finishers, expansion joint finishers,* or *concrete paving-finishing machine operators.*

Experienced masons with good judgment, planning skills, and the ability to deal with people may advance to supervisory positions. Supervisors with a broad understanding of the other construction trades may eventually become job superintendents, in charge of the whole range of activities at the job site. Cement masons may also become estimators for concrete contractors, calculating materials requirements and labor costs. Only a few cement masons decide to open their own contracting businesses, usually doing small projects like sidewalks and patios.

Employment Outlook

Employment opportunities for cement masons are expected to increase more slowly than the average for all occupations over the next ten to fifteen years. Construction activity is expected to expand during this period, and concrete will be a very important building material. Cement masons will be in demand to help build roads, bridges, buildings, and many other structures. Yet the productivity of cement masons will be improved considerably by the introduction of better equipment, tools, and materials. That is, fewer cement masons will be needed to do the same amount of work. The net effect will be that employment in this occupation will not keep up with the increasing use of concrete in construction.

Nonetheless, many new openings will arise every year as experienced workers move into other occupations or leave the labor force. In areas where the local economy is thriving and there are plenty of building projects, there may sometimes be a shortage of cement masons. At other times, even skilled masons may experience periods of unemployment because the economy is in a downturn and the level of construction activity has fallen.

Earnings

The earnings of cement masons vary widely according to factors such as geographical location, whether they do much overtime work, how much bad weather or local economic conditions reduce the hours they work, and whether they are union members. Working overtime, usually at time-and-a-half rates, is frequently possible, because once concrete has been poured, the finishing operations must be completed quickly. Nonunion workers generally have lower wage rates than union workers.

In the 1990s, most cement masons have earnings somewhere between $15,900 and $31,200 per year. A few earn over $40,000, while some make as little as about $13,100. Apprentices start at wages that are about 50 to 60 percent of a fully qualified mason's wage. They receive periodic raises, so that in the last phase of training, their wage is between 90 and 95 percent of the experienced worker's pay.

Conditions of Work

Cement masons do strenuous work, and they need to have good stamina. They stay active much of the time, especially when concrete has been poured and needs to be finished immediately. Many cement masons work outdoors. In general, concrete cannot be poured in cold or rainy weather, but temporary heated shelters are sometimes used to extend the time when work can be done. Masons work in a variety of locations, sometimes on the ground, sometimes on ladders and scaffolds. They may need to lift or push weights, and they often kneel, bend, and stoop. To protect their knees, many masons routinely wear kneepads. They may also wear water-repellent boots and protective clothing.

Common hazards on the job include falling off ladders, being hit by falling objects, muscle strains, and rough hands from contact with wet concrete. By exercising caution and following established job safety practices, cement masons can minimize their exposure to hazardous conditions.

Sources of Additional Information

■ **Associated General Contractors of America**
1957 E Street, NW
Washington, DC 20006
Tel: 202-393-2040
Email: 73264.15@compuserv.com
WWW: http://owlworld.compuserv.com/homepages/agc

■ **Canadian Masonry Contractors Association**
#201, 1013 Wilson Avenue
Downsview, ON M3K 1G1 Canada
Tel: 416-635-7179

■ **International Union of Bricklayers and Allied Craftsmen**
815 15th Street, NW
Washington, DC 20005
Tel: 202-783-3788

■ **Mason Contractors Association of America**
1550 Spring Road, Suite 320
Oak Brook, IL 60521
Tel: 630-782-6767

■ **Operative Plasterers and Cement Masons International Association of the United States and Canada**
1125 17th Street, NW
Washington, DC 20036
Tel: 202-393-6569

■ **Portland Cement Association**
5420 Old Orchard Road
Skokie, IL 60077
Tel: 847-966-6200

Civil Engineering Technicians

Definition

Civil engineering technicians help civil engineers design, plan, and build public as well as private works to meet the community's needs. They are employed in a wide range of projects, such as highways, drainage systems, water and sewage facilities, railroads, subways, airports, dams, bridges, and tunnels.

History

Engineering, both military and civil, is one of the oldest of professions. The pyramids of ancient Egypt and the bridges, roads, and aqueducts of the Roman Empire (some of which are still in use) are examples of ancient engineering feats.

Although, from earliest times, engineers have been at work building locks and dams, public buildings, cathedrals, and highways, until the nineteenth century most of the highly trained and knowledgeable engineers were military engineers. It was not until the eighteenth century in France and England that civil engineers began to organize themselves into professional societies to exchange information or plan projects. At that time, most civil engineers were still self-taught, skilled craft workers. Thomas Telford, for instance, Britain's leading road builder and first president of the Institution of Civil Engineers, started his career as a stonemason. And John Rennie, the builder of the new London Bridge, began as a millwright's apprentice.

The first major educational programs intended for civil engineers were offered by the Ecole Polytechnique, founded in Paris in 1794. Similar courses at the Bauakadamie, founded in Berlin in 1799, and at University College, London, founded in 1826, soon followed. In the United States, the first courses in civil engineering were taught at Rensselaer Polytechnic Institute, founded in 1824.

From the beginning, civil engineers have required the help of skilled assistants to handle the many details that are part of all phases of civil engineering. Traditionally, these assistants have possessed a combination of basic knowledge and good manual skills. As construction techniques have become more sophisticated, however, there is an increased need for assistants to be technically trained in specialized fields relevant to civil engineering.

These technically trained assistants are known today as civil engineering technicians. Just as separate educational programs and professional identity developed for the civil engineer in the eighteenth and nineteenth centuries, so it is for civil engineering technicians in the twentieth century. Today, the civil engineering technician is a respected member of the civil engineering team comprising scientists, engineers, technicians, technologists, and craft workers.

Nature of the Work

Civil engineering technicians work in many areas. State highway departments, for example, use their services to collect data, to design and draw plans, and to supervise the construction and maintenance of roadways. Railroad and airport facilities require similar services. Cities and counties need to have transportation systems, drainage systems, and water and sewage facilities planned, built, and maintained with the help of civil engineering technicians.

Civil engineering technicians participate in all stages of the construction process. During the planning stages, they help engineers prepare lists of materials needed and help estimate project costs. One of the most important technician positions at this stage is the *structural engineering technician.* Structural engineering technicians help engineers calculate the size, number, and composition of beams and columns, and investigate allowable soil pressures that develop from the weight of these structures. If the pressure will cause excessive settling or some other failure, they may help design special piers, rafts, pilings, or footings to prevent structural problems.

During the planning stages, civil engineering technicians help engineers prepare drawings, maps, and charts; during the actual construction phase, *construction technicians* assist building contractors and site supervisors in preparing work schedules and cost estimates and in performing work inspections. One of their most important duties is to ensure that each step of construction is completed before workers arrive to begin the next stage.

Some technicians specialize in certain types of construction projects. *Highway technicians,* for example, perform surveys and cost estimates as well as plan and supervise highway construction and maintenance. *Rail and waterway technicians* survey, make specifications and cost estimates, and help plan and construct railway and waterway facilities. *Assistant city engineers* coordinate the planning and construction of city streets, sewers, drainage systems, refuse facilities, and other major civil projects.

Other technicians specialize in certain phases of the construction process. For example, *construction materials testing technicians* sample and run tests on rock, soil, cement, asphalt, wood, steel, concrete, and other materials. *Photogrammetric technicians* use aerial photographs to prepare maps, plans, and profiles. *Party chiefs* work for licensed land surveyors, survey land for boundary-line locations, and plan subdivisions and other large-area land developments.

There are other specialized positions for civil engineering technicians: *research engineering technicians* test and develop new products and equipment; *sales engineering technicians* sell building materials, construction equipment, and engineering services; and *water resources technicians* gather data, make computations and drawings for water projects, and prepare economic studies.

Requirements

A student thinking of a career in civil engineering needs a desire to be a builder or planner, an understanding of mathematics and sciences, an ability to get along with others, an aptitude for learning, and the ability to think and plan ahead.

Students should take all the mathematics, science, and communications subjects available to them in high school. In general, they should follow the course for admission into an institution offering either a two- or four-year degree in civil engineering technology.

Helpful classes include mathematics (with at least two years of algebra, plane and solid geometry, and trigonometry); physics (with laboratory experience); chemistry; biology; and any other science courses.

Because the ability to read and interpret material is very important, four years of English and language skills courses are basic requirements. Reports and letters are an essential part of the technician's work, so a firm grasp of English grammar is important.

Other useful courses include mechanical drawing and shop courses. Civil engineering technicians often make use of mechanical drawings to convey their ideas to others, and neat, well-executed drawings are important to convey a sense of accuracy and competence.

Students should be careful to choose a school that offers an accredited program in civil engineering technology. In such programs, more mathematics and science subjects, including physics, will be studied to prepare the student for later specialty courses, such as surveying, materials, hydraulics, highway and bridge construction and design, structures, railway and water systems, heavy construction, soils, steel and concrete construction, cost and estimates, and management and construction technology. Students should also take courses in computer programming and photogrammetry.

A great deal of the student's time will be spent in laboratory and field study in these specialties. This hands-on experience prepares technicians for their special role in the civil engineering team.

In addition, drafting procedures and techniques will be developed and polished in intermediate and advanced-level courses. Courses in human relations, economics, and professional ethics are available and recommended. English is the most important of the nontechnical subjects, as technicians need to convey their thoughts to others. Courses in public speaking and report writing are also a good idea.

To advance in professional standing, civil engineering technicians should try to become a Certified Engineering Technician. Civil engineering technicians may, upon completion of the required years of service, take an examination for licensing as a Licensed Land Surveyor. The application to take the exam is very stringent, and not all who apply qualify for the exam. Successful completion of this exam enables technicians to operate their own surveying businesses.

Opportunities for Experience & Exploration

One of the best ways to acquire firsthand experience in this field is through part-time or summer work with a construction company. Even if the job is menial, you can still observe surveying teams, site supervisors, building inspectors, skilled craft workers, and civil engineering technicians at work. If such work is not possible, students can organize field trips to various construction sites or to facilities where building materials are manufactured.

Courses in shop and drafting will also provide future technicians with excellent opportunities to sample some of the work they may be doing later.

Methods of Entering

Most students receive assistance from their school to find jobs upon graduation. Most schools maintain placement offices, which many prospective employers contact when they have job openings. The placement offices, in turn, help the student or graduate prepare a resume of relevant school and work experiences and usually arrange personal interviews with prospective employers.

Many schools also have cooperative work-study programs with particular companies and government agencies. Under such a program, the company or government agency often becomes the new technician's place of full-time employment after graduation.

Some students make use of state and private employment services with job listings in this field. Others consult want ads or write directly to possible future employers. Students should also take every opportunity to meet and get to know people in the field. Such people often know about present and future job openings and can pass the word along to interested newcomers.

Advancement

Civil engineering technicians must study and learn throughout their careers. They must learn new techniques, master the operation of new equipment, and gain greater depth of knowledge in their chosen fields to keep themselves abreast of the latest developments. Some technicians move on to supervisory positions, while others get additional education and become civil engineers. A few of the opportunities for technicians with advanced education and degrees, skills, and experience follows.

Associate municipal designers direct workers to prepare design drawings and feasibility studies for dams and municipal water and sewage plants. *Associate structures designers* direct workers to prepare design drawings and cost estimates of structural features, such as foundations, columns, piers, and beams. *City or county building inspectors* review and then approve or reject plans for construction of large buildings. *City and county engineers* operate, plan, and direct engineering or public works departments. *Licensed land surveyors* operate land surveying businesses as owners or partners. *Photogrammetrists* direct the preparation of maps and charts from aerial photography. *Project engineers,* or *resident engineers,* supervise a number of projects and field parties for city, county, or state highway departments. Finally, some technicians go on to become construction superintendents or even owners of their own construction company, supply company, or laboratory testing company.

Employment Outlook

The employment outlook for civil engineering technicians is good. Although the total amount of civil construction may be affected by general economic conditions and levels of government spending, there will remain a need for more technicians to assist civil engineers and to relieve them of any duties that may be delegated. Despite short-term or even protracted periods of economic dislocation, there will remain needs for construction projects that address the problems of urban redevelopment, water shortages, transportation systems, industrial waste pollution, and traffic congestion.

Earnings

Civil engineering technicians usually begin their first jobs at a salary range of about $16,500 to $29,000 a year, with the higher paying jobs going to those with advanced education. Most experienced technicians earn between $33,000 to $49,390 or more per year. Some senior technicians earn as much as $71,500 a year or more.

The incomes of many civil engineering technicians who operate their own construction, surveying, or equipment businesses are good. Some of these companies can earn millions of dollars each year.

As in all industries, paid vacations, pension plans, and insurance are normal parts of the benefits paid to civil engineering technicians. Many companies pay the superintendent a bonus if a job is completed ahead of schedule or if the job is completed for less than the estimated cost. These bonuses sometimes amount to more than the employee's regular annual salary.

Conditions of Work

Technicians usually work forty hours a week with extra pay for overtime. Working conditions vary from job to job: technicians who enjoy being outdoors may choose a job in construction or surveying; those who prefer working indoors may work in a consulting engineer's office on computations, drafting, or design, or on map plotting, materials testing, or making calculations from field notes and tests. In either case, the work done by civil engineering technicians is usually cleaner than the work done by most other construction trades workers.

Civil engineering technicians feel the pride that comes from being a member of a team that constructs major buildings, bridges, or dams. In a way, such projects become monuments to the efforts of each member of the team. And there is the accompanying satisfaction that the project has improved, if only in a modest way, the quality of life in a community.

Sources of Additional Information

■ **American Congress on Surveying and Mapping**
5410 Grosvenor Lane
Bethesda, MD 20814-2122
Tel: 301-493-0200

■ **American Society for Engineering Education**
11 Dupont Circle, Suite 200
Washington, DC 20036
Tel: 202-331-3500
WWW: http://www.asee.org

■ **American Society of Certified Engineering Technicians**
PO Box 1348
Flowery Branch, GA 30542
Tel: 404-967-9173

■ **American Society of Civil Engineers**
345 East 47th Street
New York, NY 10017
Tel: 212-705-7496

Construction Inspectors

School Subjects
Mathematics
Shop (Trade/Vo-tech education)

Personal Interests
Building things
Fixing things

Work Environment
Indoors and outdoors
Primarily multiple locations

Minimum Education Level
High school diploma

Salary Range
$17,500 to $41,000

Certification or Licensing
Recommended

Outlook
Faster than the average

DOT: 182   **GOE:** 05.03.06   **NOC:** 2264

Definition

Construction inspectors work for federal, state, and local governments. Their job is to examine the construction, alteration, or repair of highways, streets, sewer and water systems, dams, bridges, buildings, and other structures to ensure that they comply with the building codes and ordinances, zoning regulations, and contract specifications.

History

Construction is one of the major industries of the modern world. Public construction includes structures such as public housing projects, schools, hospitals, administrative and service buildings, industrial and military facilities, highways, and sewer and water systems.

ction Inspectors

To ensure the safety of the public's use of buildings, highways, streets, and other structures and systems, various governing bodies establish building codes that contractors must follow. It is the job of the construction inspector to ensure that the codes are properly followed.

Nature of the Work

This occupation is made up of four broad categories of specialization: building, electrical, mechanical, and public works. *Building inspectors* examine the structural quality of buildings. They check the plans before construction, visit the work site a number of times during construction, and make a final inspection when the project is completed. Some building inspectors specialize in areas such as structural steel or reinforced concrete buildings.

Electrical inspectors visit work sites to inspect the installation of electrical systems and equipment. They check wiring, lighting, generators, and sound and security systems. They may also inspect the wiring for elevators, heating and air-conditioning systems, kitchen appliances, and other electrical installations.

Mechanical inspectors inspect plumbing systems and the mechanical components of heating and air-conditioning equipment and kitchen appliances. They also examine gas tanks, piping, and gas-fired appliances. Some mechanical inspectors specialize in elevators, plumbing, or boilers.

Elevator inspectors inspect both the mechanical and the electrical features of lifting and conveying devices, such as elevators, escalators, and moving sidewalks. They also test their speed, load allowances, brakes, and safety devices.

Plumbing inspectors inspect plumbing installations, water supply systems, drainage and sewer systems, water heater installations, fire sprinkler systems, and air and gas piping systems; they also examine building sites for soil type to determine water table level, seepage rate, and other conditions.

Heating and refrigeration inspectors examine heating, ventilating, air-conditioning, and refrigeration installations in new buildings and approve alteration plans for those elements in existing buildings.

Public works inspectors make sure that government construction of water and sewer systems, highways, streets, bridges, and dams conforms to contract specifications. They visit work sites to inspect excavations, mixing and pouring of concrete, and asphalt paving. They also keep records of the amount of work performed and the materials used so that proper payment can be made. These inspectors may specialize in highways, reinforced concrete, or ditches.

Construction inspectors use measuring devices and other test equipment, take photographs, keep a daily log of their work, and write reports. If any detail of a project does not comply with the various codes, ordinances, or contract specifications, or if construction is being done without proper permits, the inspectors have the authority to issue a stop-work order.

Requirements

People interested in construction inspection must be high school graduates who have taken courses in drafting, algebra, geometry, and English. Employers prefer graduates of an apprenticeship program or a community or junior college or people with at least two years toward an engineering or architectural degree. Required courses include construction technology, blueprint reading, technical math, English, and building inspection.

Most construction inspectors have several years' experience either as a construction contractor or supervisor, or as a craft or trade worker such as carpenter, electrician, plumber, or pipefitter. This experience shows a knowledge of construction materials and practices, which is necessary in inspections.

Construction inspectors receive most of their training on the job. The first two weeks or so are spent under the supervision of an experienced inspector. Then the new inspector is put to work on a simple project, such as a residence, and is gradually advanced to more complex types of construction.

Some states require certification for employment. Inspectors can earn a certificate by passing examinations on construction techniques, materials, and code requirements. The exams are offered by three model code organizations: the International Conference of Building Officials; Building Officials and Code Administrators International; and Southern Building Code Congress International.

Construction inspectors are expected to have a valid driver's license because they must be able to travel to and from the construction sites. They must also pass a civil service exam.

Opportunities for Experience & Exploration

Field trips to construction sites and interviews with contractors or building trade officials are good ways to gain practical information about what it is like to work in the industry and how best to prepare for it.

Summer jobs at a construction site provide an overview of the work involved in a building project. Students may also seek part-time jobs with a general contracting company, with a specialized contractor (such as a plumbing or electrical contractor), or as a carpenter's helper. Jobs in certain supply houses will help students become familiar with the materials used in construction.

Methods of Entering

People right out of high school usually enter the construction industry as a trainee or apprentice. Information about these programs may be obtained from local contractors, building trade unions, or school vocational counselors. Graduates of technical schools or colleges of construction and engineering may expect to start work as an engineering aide, drafter, estimator, or assistant engineer.

Jobs may be found through school placement offices, employment agencies, and unions or by applying directly to contracting company personnel offices. Application may also be made directly to the employment offices of the federal, state, or local government.

Advancement

An engineering degree is usually required to become a supervisory inspector.

The federal, state, and large city governments provide formal training programs for their construction inspectors to keep them abreast of new building code developments and to broaden their knowledge of construction materials, practices, and inspection techniques. Inspectors for small agencies can upgrade their skills by attending state-conducted training programs or taking college or correspondence courses.

Employment Outlook

In the 1990s, federal, state, and local governments employ about 60,000 construction and building inspectors in the United States; more than half of these inspectors work in municipal and county building departments. Large inspection staffs are employed by cities and suburbs that are experiencing rapid growth. Federal inspectors may work for such agencies as the Department of Defense or the Departments of Housing and Urban Development, Agriculture, and the Interior.

The demand for government construction inspectors through the year 2000 is expected to grow faster than the average rate for all occupations. There will likely be increased construction activity, as well as a rising concern for public safety and improved quality of construction. Some responsibilities handled by inspectors will be assumed by engineers, construction managers, and maintenance supervisors. The level of new construction fluctuates with the economy, but maintenance and renovation continue during the downswings, so inspectors are rarely laid off.

Earnings

In the 1990s, inspectors make an average of $29,200 a year. Salaries range between $17,500 and $41,000. Building inspectors earn slightly more than other inspectors. Salaries are slightly higher in the North and West than in the South and are considerably higher in large metropolitan areas. Inspectors who work for the federal government in the 1990s earn an average annual salary of $26,100.

Conditions of Work

Construction inspectors work both indoors and outdoors, dividing their time between their offices and the work sites. Inspection sites are dirty and cluttered with tools, machinery, and debris. Although the work is not considered hazardous, inspectors must climb ladders and stairs and crawl under buildings.

The hours are usually regular, but when there is an accident at a site, the inspector has to remain on the job until reports have been completed. The work is steady year-round, not seasonal as are some other construction occupations. In slow construction periods, the inspectors are kept busy examining the renovation of older buildings.

Sources of Additional Information

■ **Building Officials and Code Administrators International**
4051 West Flossmoor Road
Country Club Hills, IL 60478
Tel: 708-799-2300

■ **Canadian Construction Association**
65 Albert Street, 10th Floor
Ottawa, ON K1P 6A4 Canada
Tel: 613-236-9455

■ **International Conference of Building Officials**
5360 South Workman Mill Road
Whittier, CA 90601
Tel: 310-699-0541

■ **Southern Building Code Congress International**
900 Montclair Road
Birmingham, AL 35213
Tel: 205-591-1853

Construction Laborers

School Subjects
Mathematics
Shop (Trade/Vo-tech education)

Personal Interests
Building things
Fixing things

Work Environment
Primarily multiple locations
Indoors and outdoors

Minimum Education Level
High school diploma
Apprenticeship

Salary Range
$16,000 to $29,000+

Certification or Licensing
None

Outlook
As fast as the average

DOT: 869   **GOE:** 05.10.01   **NOC:** 7611

Definition

Construction laborers do a variety of tasks at construction sites of buildings, highways, bridges, and other public and private building projects. Depending on the type of project, construction laborers may carry materials used by craft workers, clean up debris, operate cement mixers, or lay and seal together lengths of sewer pipe. They are also involved in hazardous waste/environmental remediation.

History

In the past, when people wanted simple structures built, they may well have done the work themselves. But inevitably the larger, more complex structures required the efforts of many workers. These workers included both skilled specialists in certain activities and others who assisted the specialists or did numerous other less complicated but necessary physical tasks. Today the people who provide this kind of aid may be called construction laborers. Their work usually does not require great skill, but it is essential to getting the job done.

Nature of the Work

Construction laborers are employed on all kinds of construction jobs, such as building bridges, viaducts, piers, office and apartment buildings, highways, streets, pipelines, railroads, river and harbor projects, sewers, tunnels, and waterworks. Many laborers are employed by private firms that contract to do these construction jobs. Others work for state or local governments on public works or for utility companies in such activities as road repair. Construction laborers are also involved in building remodeling, demolition, and repair work.

At the direction of supervisors or other skilled workers, construction laborers perform a wide variety of duties, such as loading and unloading materials, erecting and dismantling scaffolding, digging and leveling dirt and gravel, wrecking old buildings, removing rubble, pouring and spreading concrete and asphalt, removing forms from set concrete, and carrying supplies to building craft workers. They may use equipment ranging from ordinary picks and shovels to various kinds of machines used in construction, such as air hammers or pile-driving equipment.

On some jobs, laborers are assigned to one type of routine task; on other jobs, they are rotated through different tasks as the job progresses. Some laborers tend to work in one branch of the construction industry, such as laying pipelines or building roads. Others transfer from one area of construction to another depending mainly on the availability of work.

To do their job well, some construction laborers may need to be familiar with the duties of skilled craft workers as well as a variety of tools, machines, materials, and methods used at the job site. Some laborers do work that requires a considerable amount of know-how, such as those who work with the explosives used to break up bedrock before excavation work can begin on some construction projects. These workers must know how different kinds of explosives can be used safely, avoiding both injury and property damage. Another example of laborers who need specialized knowledge are those who work in pressurized areas while constructing dam and bridge foundations. Laborers in these kinds of special situations are usually trained on the job by their supervisors.

Requirements

Construction work is strenuous, so employers seek workers who are physically fit enough to do the job. Laborers usually must be at least eighteen years old and reliable, hard-working, and able to follow oral and written instructions.

Some employers prefer high school graduates. In general, no particular training is necessary for most entry-level construction laborer jobs. Beginners learn whatever job skills they need informally as they work under the supervision of more experienced workers. Those who must work with potentially dangerous equipment or materials receive instruction in safety procedures that minimize the chance of accidents.

Apprenticeship training is also available for those seeking more structured, thorough training in this field. Apprenticeship programs include 5,058 to 6,148 hours of on-the-job and classroom instruction in such areas as site and project preparation and maintenance; tools, equipment, and materials; safety; environmental remediation; building construction; and heavy/highway construction. Apprentices receive specific training and instruction in dealing with the removal of asbestos, hazardous waste, lead, radiation, and underground storage tanks, as well as the basics of working with asphalt, concrete, lines and grades, masonry, and pipe laying, and in reading blueprints.

Opportunities for Experience & Exploration

People who are interested in this work can often get summer jobs as laborers on building or construction projects. This is the best kind of experience students can have to help them evaluate their interest and potential in this field. They may also benefit by talking to local contractors or to local officials of the Laborers' International Union of North America, a union to which many laborers belong.

Methods of Entering

The usual first step in getting a job in this field is applying directly to a construction contractor or to the local office of the Laborers' International Union. Good leads for jobs may be found through the state employment service and the classified sections of local newspapers. Workers who have completed a construction craftworker apprenticeship program usually are considered first for job openings above those applicants who have no prior experience.

Advancement

Without additional training, construction laborers have limited opportunities for advancement. Some laborers move into jobs as mechanics or skilled operators of construction equipment. Workers who show responsibility and good judgment may be promoted to supervisory positions.

Employment Outlook

A moderate increase is predicted for the next ten to fifteen years in the total volume of construction activity nationwide. However, job opportunities for laborers will probably change at about the same rate as jobs in other occupations. Certain technological developments, such as more efficient grading machinery and mechanical lifting devices, may mean that the rate of increase in employment of construction laborers will not be as great as the expected increase in construction activity. The level of construction activity is always affected by local economic conditions. Regions that are prosperous will offer better job possibilities for construction laborers than areas where the economy is not expanding.

Nonetheless, this is a large employment field and turnover is high among laborers. For these reasons, every year there will be many new job openings, mainly in connection with large projects, because employers need to replace those workers who have changed jobs or left the labor force.

Earnings

Construction workers often receive substantial hourly wages, but the hourly rates are often poor indicators of annual earnings. The seasonal nature of construction work and time lost because of other factors can significantly reduce the total income of construction workers. There is also a great difference in the wages paid to construction laborers in different parts of the country. Pay is higher for laborers with certain kinds of special experience or doing certain kinds of tasks. Overall, in the 1990s, laborers who are employed full time earn roughly between $16,000 to $29,000 or more per year.

Conditions of Work

Construction laborers do heavy physical work. They may need to lift heavy weights, kneel, crouch, stoop, crawl, or work in awkward positions. Much of the job is outdoors, sometimes in hot or cold weather, in wind or rain, in dust, mud, noise, or other uncomfortable conditions. Laborers may be exposed to fumes, odors, dangerous particles, or irritating chemicals. They need to be constantly aware of danger and must always be careful to observe good safety practices. They often wear gloves, hats, and eye, mouth, or hearing protection to help avoid injury.

Although laborers can have good earnings during some periods, the industry is subject to ups and downs, and workers need to plan for periods of low earnings. People who are able to go where the jobs are can be more steadily employed. In general, most jobs are located in more densely populated and industrialized sections of the country.

Work schedules, weather conditions, or other factors may require night or weekend shifts and sometimes hours beyond the standard forty-hour week.

Sources of Additional Information

■ **Associated General Contractors of America**
1957 E Street, NW
Washington, DC 20006
Tel: 202-393-2040
Email: 73264.15@compuserv.com
WWW: http://agc.org

■ **Laborers' International Union of North America**
905 16th Street, NW
Washington, DC 20006
Tel: 202-737-8320

41

Cost Estimators

Definition

Cost estimators compile cost and price data and use standard estimating techniques to prepare estimates of the cost of construction or manufacturing projects. They conduct feasibility studies to help contractors, owners, or other project planners determine how much a project or product will cost and if it is economically viable.

History

People in business need to be able to predict how much a future project, process, or product will cost to determine what they can charge the customer in return. No effective business operation can be undertaken without a thorough assessment of the potential costs. This information helps management best allocate resources to make a profit for the company.

Manufacturers usually need to estimate production (operating) costs (for example, costs for assembly line or other operations that are repeated). As production techniques become more specialized, it has become necessary to have specialists responsible for collecting and analyzing cost information on the many facets of production. Costs of labor, materials, transportation, equipment, and many other factors all must be collected and interpreted before a manufacturing decision can be made. The cost estimator fulfills this function and is the vital link between a product idea and its implementation.

In construction, preliminary, bid authorization, and check estimates are made to determine construction or building costs. As long as there are buildings to be constructed, there will be a continuing need for experts who can establish how much a project will cost so that the people paying for the project will be able to make wise business decisions and plan accordingly.

Nature of the Work

Cost estimators collect and analyze information on various factors influencing costs, such as the labor, materials, and machinery needed for a particular project. Cost estimators generally work in one of two areas—construction or manufacturing—although all types of businesses ultimately need someone who can effectively estimate costs related to the scope of the particular business.

In the construction industry, the nature of the work is largely determined by the type and size of the project being estimated. On a large building project, for example, the estimator reviews architectural drawings and other bidding documents before any construction begins. Then the estimator visits the potential construction site to collect site development information that may affect the way the structure is built. After compiling thorough research on the construction process and the people involved, the estimator writes a quantity survey, or "takeoff," by completing standard estimating forms or using a computer spreadsheet.

Sometimes more than one estimator is used on a project, and estimators may specialize in one area. For example, one estimator may assess the electrical costs of a project while another concentrates on the transportation or insurance costs of that same project. It is then the responsibility of a *chief estimator* to combine the reports and submit one development proposal.

In both construction and manufacturing, the cost estimator's role is to bring together complex data in assessing costs. For example, in the manufacturing process, an estimator may work with engineers to develop visual aids, such as charts, showing that labor quantities (and therefore costs) should go down as the project progresses because the workers will learn the manufacturing process, become more efficient, and thereby increase productivity. Charts may be used to measure how prices for a particular part compare with prices paid in the past and what can be expected to be paid in the future.

An estimator must know current prices for labor, materials, and other factors that influence costs. This data is obtained by calling vendors to obtain quotes and using commercial price books and catalogs. An estimator should also be able to compute and understand accounting and mathematical formulas and be able to make sound decisions based on these computations. Computers are frequently used to do the routine calculations, leaving the estimator more time to analyze data and evaluate effective production techniques.

Requirements

Construction and manufacturing firms usually prefer estimators to have experience with their procedures and a thorough knowledge of the costs involved in production. To prepare for this on-the-job training, a high school student should take courses in accounting and mathematics. English courses and courses in writing are also recommended. Postsecondary two-year training programs, such as those offered at community colleges or technical schools, are also helpful. Course work should include physics and technical drawing, as well as specific courses covering manufacturing and construction processes.

Some employers request that an entry-level estimator have a bachelor's degree in civil engineering or mathematics. For example, the federal government will only accept entry-level applicants with a college degree. More than two hundred colleges and universities in the United States offer four-year degrees in building construction or construction technology, which teach basic construction estimating.

Although there are no licensing requirements, many cost estimators find it helpful to become certified. To become certified, an estimator must have between three and seven years of experience in the field and pass a written and/or oral test. Information on certification procedures and other professional training is available from organizations such as the American Society of Professional Estimators and the Society of Cost Estimating Analysis.

Opportunities for Experience & Exploration

Experience is especially important in a field such as this, with so much emphasis on on-the-job training. Part-time work with a construction crew or manufacturing firm, especially during the busy summer months, is a good way to gain experience. Talking with those in the field is another way of finding out about career opportunities.

Methods of Entering

Many cost estimators are tradespeople who display a particular aptitude or interest for cost analysis. For example, an experienced plumber may become an estimator on the contracting projects done by the company. Other people complete a two-year training program or bachelor's degree and then enter the workforce. School placement offices can be good sources of employment leads for recent graduates. Applying directly to manufacturers, construction firms, and government agencies is another route.

Advancement

As in many professions, promotions for cost estimators are dependent on skill and experience. Advancement usually comes in the way of more responsibility and higher wages. A skilled cost estimator at a large construction company may become a chief estimator. Some experienced cost estimators also go into consulting work.

Employment Outlook

As in most industries, highly trained college graduates and those with the most experience have the best job prospects. Employment for cost estimators is expected to increase about as fast as the average through the 1990s. Many cost estimators work in the construction field, where employment depends on the amount of construction that takes place. Residential construction is expected to slow over the next decade, but commercial and industrial buildings should pick up the slack.

Earnings

Salaries vary according to the size of the construction or manufacturing firm and the experience and education of the worker. Average starting salaries range between $16,000 and $24,000 a year. Those with college degrees can earn up to $30,000 in their beginning years. Very experienced cost estimators earn as much as $75,000 annually. Those with certification should earn between $30,000 and $60,000 per year, and some specialists make even more.

Conditions of Work

Much of the work takes place in a typical office setting, with accounting records and other information close by. However, estimators visit construction sites or manufacturing facilities to inspect production procedures. Often the work entails consulting with engineers, work supervisors, and other professionals involved in the production or manufacturing process. Estimators usually work a forty-hour week, although longer hours may be required if a project is on deadline. Overtime hours almost always occur in the summer when construction projects are in full force.

Estimators should be able to work long hours collecting and analyzing complex economic data. They should be well organized and be able to work under deadline pressure.

Sources of Additional Information

■ **AACE International**
PO Box 1557
Morgantown, WV 26507
Tel: 304-296-8444

■ **American Society of Professional Estimators**
11141 Georgia Avenue, Suite 412
Wheaton, MD 20902
Tel: 301-929-8848

■ **Society of Cost Estimating Analysis**
101 South Whiting Street, Suite 313
Alexandria, VA 22304
Tel: 703-751-8069

Drafters

School Subjects
Mathematics
Shop (Trade/Vo-tech Education)

Personal Interests
Building things
Drawing/painting

Work Environment
Primarily indoors
Primarily one location

Minimum Education Level
Some postsecondary training
Apprenticeship

Salary Range
$18,000 to $45,000

Certification or Licensing
None

Outlook
More slowly than the average

DOT: 017   **GOE:** 05.03.02   **NOC:** 2253

Definition

The *drafter* prepares working plans and detail drawings of products or structures from the rough sketches, specifications, and calculations of engineers, architects, and designers. These drawings are used in engineering or manufacturing to reproduce exactly the product or structure according to the specified dimensions. The drafter uses knowledge of various machines, engineering practices, mathematics, building materials, and other physical sciences to complete the drawings.

History

In industry, drafting is the conversion of ideas from people's minds to precise working specifications from which products can be made. Many people find it much easier to give directions by drawing than by telling or writing and to assemble new equipment if the instructions include diagrams and drawings. Industry has come to rely on drafters to develop the working specifications from the new ideas and findings of those in the laboratories, shops, and factories.

Nature of the Work

The drafter prepares detailed plans and specification drawings from the ideas, notes, or rough sketches of scientists, engineers, architects, and designers. Sometimes drawings are developed after a visit to a project in the field or as the result of a discussion with one or more people involved in the job. The drawings, which usually provide a number of different views of the object, must be exact and accurate. They vary greatly in size depending on the type of drawing. Some assembly drawings, often called "layouts," are twenty-five to thirty feet long, while others are very small. Drawings must contain enough detail, whatever their size, so that the part, object, or building can be constructed from them. Such drawings usually include information concerning the quality of materials to be used, their cost, and the processes to be followed in carrying out the job. In developing their drawings made to scale of the object to be built, drafters use a variety of instruments, such as protractors, compasses, triangles, squares, drawing pens, and pencils.

Drafters are often classified according to the type of work they do or the level of responsibility. *Senior drafters* use the preliminary information and ideas provided by engineers and architects to make design layouts. They may have the title of *chief drafter* and assign work to other drafters and supervise their activities. *Detailers* make complete drawings, giving dimensions, material, and any other necessary information of each part shown on the layout. *Checkers* carefully examine drawings to check for errors in computing or in recording dimensions and specifications. *Tracers,* who are usually *assistant drafters,* make corrections and prepare drawings for reproduction by tracing them on transparent cloth, paper, or plastic film.

Drafters may also specialize in a particular field of work, such as mechanical, electrical, electronic, aeronautical, structural, or architectural drafting.

Although the nature of the work of drafters is not too different from one specialization to another, there is a considerable variation in the type of object with which they deal.

Commercial drafters do all-around drafting, such as plans for building sites, layouts of offices and factories, and drawings of charts, forms, and records. *Computer-assisted drafters* use computers to make drawings and layouts for such fields as aeronautics, architecture, or electronics.

Civil drafters make construction drawings for roads and highways, river and harbor improvements, flood control, drainage, and other civil engineering projects. *Structural drafters* draw plans for bridge trusses, plate girders, roof trusses, trestle bridges, and other structures that use structural reinforcing steel, concrete, masonry, and other structural materials.

Cartographic drafters prepare maps of geographic areas to show natural and constructed features, political boundaries, and other features. Topographical drafters draft and correct maps from original sources, such as other maps, surveying notes, and aerial photographs.

Architectural drafters draw plans of buildings, including artistic and structural features. *Landscape drafters* make detailed drawings from sketches furnished by landscape architects.

Heating and ventilating drafters draft plans for heating, air-conditioning, ventilating, and sometimes refrigeration equipment. *Plumbing drafters* draw diagrams for the installation of plumbing equipment.

Mechanical drafters make working drawings of machinery, automobiles, power plants, or any mechanical device. *Castings drafters* prepare detailed drawings of castings, which are objects formed in a mold. *Tool design drafters* draft manufacturing plans for all kinds of tools. *Patent drafters* make drawings of mechanical devices for use by lawyers to obtain patent rights for their clients.

Electrical drafters make schematics and wiring diagrams to be used by construction crews working on equipment and wiring in power plants, communications centers, buildings, or electrical distribution systems.

Electronics drafters draw schematics and wiring diagrams for television cameras and TV sets, radio transmitters and receivers, computers, radiation detectors, and other electronic equipment.

Electromechanisms design drafters draft designs of electromechanical equipment such as aircraft engines, data processing systems, gyroscopes, automatic materials handling and processing machinery, or biomedical equipment. *Electromechanical drafters* draw wiring diagrams, layouts, and mechanical details for the electrical components and systems of a mechanical process or device.

Aeronautical drafters prepare engineering drawings for planes, missiles, and spacecraft. *Automotive design drafters* and *automotive design layout drafters* both turn out working layouts and master drawings of components, assemblies, and systems of automobiles and other vehicles. Automotive design drafters make original designs from specifications, and automotive design layout drafters make drawings based on prior layouts or sketches.

Marine drafters draft the structural and mechanical features of ships, docks, and marine buildings and equipment. Projects range from petroleum drilling platforms to nuclear submarines.

49

Geological drafters make diagrams and maps of geological formations and locations of mineral, oil, and gas deposits. *Geophysical drafters* draw maps and diagrams based on data from petroleum prospecting instruments such as seismographs, gravity meters, and magnetometers. *Directional survey drafters* plot boreholes for oil and gas wells. *Oil and gas drafters* draft plans for the construction and operation of oil fields, refineries, and pipeline systems.

A design team working on electrical or gas power plants and substations may be headed by a *chief design drafter,* who oversees architectural, electrical, mechanical, and structural drafters. Estimators and drafters draw specifications and instructions for installing voltage transformers, cables, and other electrical equipment that delivers electric power to consumers.

Requirements

Interested high school students should take science and mathematics courses, mechanical drawing (minimum of one to two years), and wood, metal, or electric shop. They also should take English and social studies classes.

Preparation beyond high school should include courses in the physical sciences, mathematics, drawing, sketching and drafting techniques, and in other technical areas essential for certain types of beginning positions and for advancement to positions of greater salary and more responsibility. This training comes through apprenticeships, junior colleges, or technical institute programs. Apprenticeship programs usually run three to four years. During this period, the apprentice works on the job and is required to take related classroom work in theory and practice.

Students interested in drafting should have a good sense of space perception (ability to visualize objects in two or three dimensions); form perception (ability to compare and to discriminate between shapes, lines, forms, and shadings); and coordinated eye-finger-hand movements.

Opportunities for Experience & Exploration

High school programs provide several opportunities for gaining experience in drafting. Mechanical drawing is a good course to take. There are also many hobbies and leisure time activities, such as woodworking, building models, and any repairing or remodeling projects, that require the preparation of drawings or use of blueprints. After the completion of some courses in mechanical drawing, it may be possible to locate a part-time or summer job in drafting.

Methods of Entering

Beginning drafters should have graduated from a post-high school program at a technical institute or a junior college. School placement offices can assist graduates in finding first jobs. Applicants for government positions may need to take a civil service examination. Those wishing to enter the field through an apprenticeship program can get information from a school counselor, a mechanical drawing or shop instructor, a local union, or from local, state, or national apprenticeship training representatives.

Beginning or inexperienced drafters often start as tracers. Students with some formal post-high school technical training often qualify for positions as junior drafters who revise detail drawings and gradually assume assignments of a more complex drawing nature.

Advancement

With additional experience and skill, beginning drafters become checkers, detailers, design drafters, or senior drafters. Movement from one to another of these job classifications is not restricted; each business must modify work assignments based on its own needs.

Drafters often move into related positions. Some typical positions include technical report writers, sales engineers, engineering assistants, production foremen, and installation technicians.

Employment Outlook

Almost four hundred thousand drafters are employed in business, industry, and government positions. About one-third work for engineering and architectural companies, and another third work for manufacturers of machinery, electrical equipment, fabricated metals, and other durable goods. Other industries that employ drafters include construction, communications, transportation, and utilities. About 7 percent of drafters work for government agencies, most of them at the state and local level. The majority of the federal government drafters work for the Department of Defense.

Employment of drafters is expected to grow more slowly than other occupations through the year 2005, despite the anticipated expansion of technological and scientific processes. New products and processes of more complex design will call for more drafting services, as will the general growth of industry. However, the increased use of computer-aided design (CAD) systems is expected to offset some of the demand, particularly for lower-level drafters who do routine work. CAD equipment can produce more and better variations of a design, which could stimulate additional activity in the field and create opportunities for drafters who are willing to switch to the new techniques.

Employment trends for drafters fluctuate with the economy. In the event of a recession, fewer buildings and manufactured products are designed, which could reduce the need for drafters in architectural, engineering, and manufacturing firms.

Earnings

In private industry, the average starting salary for drafters is about $18,000. Experienced drafters earn between $20,000 and $40,000, with the average salary at about $30,000. Senior drafters can make up to $45,000.

Conditions of Work

The drafter usually works in a well-lighted, air-conditioned, quiet room. This may be a central drafting room where drafters work side by side at large, tilted drawing tables. Some drafters work in an individual department, like engineering, research, or development, where they work alone or with other drafters and with engineers, designers, or scientists. Occasionally, drafters may need to visit other departments or construction sites to consult with engineers or to gain firsthand information.

Most drafters work a forty-hour week with little overtime. Drafters work at drawing tables for long periods of time at arrangements that require undivided concentration, close eyework, and very precise and accurate computations and drawings. There is generally little pressure, but occasionally last-minute design changes or a rush order may necessitate a deadline.

Sources of Additional Information

■ **American Design Drafting Association**
PO Box 799
Rockville, MD 20848
Tel: 301-460-6875

■ **International Federation of Professional and Technical Engineers**
8701 Georgia Avenue, Suite 701
Silver Spring, MD 20910
Tel: 301-565-9016

■ **Manitoba Society of Certified Engineering Technicians and Technologists**
602-1661 Portage Avenue
Winnipeg, MB R3J 3T7 Canada
Tel: 204-783-0088
Email: cttam@mts.net

■ **National Association of Trade and Technical Schools**
PO Box 2006
Department BL
Annapolis Junction, MD 20701

Drywall Installers and Finishers

School Subjects
Mathematics
Shop (Trade/Vo-tech education)

Personal Interests
Building things
Drawing/painting

Work Environment
Primarily indoors
Primarily multiple locations

Minimum Education Level
High school diploma
Apprenticeship

Salary Range
$20,000 to $40,000+

Certification or Licensing
None

Outlook
About as fast as the average

DOT: 840   **GOE:** 05.05.04   **NOC:** 7284

Definition

Drywall installers and *drywall finishers* plan and carry out the installation of drywall panels on interior wall and ceiling surfaces of residential, commercial, and industrial buildings.

History

Well before the invention of writing, people used trowel-like tools to plaster wet clay over the walls of crude shelters in an attempt to keep out the wind and the rain. When the Great Pyramid of Cheops was built nearly forty-five hundred years ago, the Egyptians used a gypsum plaster in decorating the surfaces of its interior passages and rooms. But gypsum plaster is difficult to work with, because it may hard-

54

en before it can be properly applied. It was not until around 1900 that additives began to be used to control the setting time of gypsum, thus opening the door for modern plastering techniques and products.

Drywall panels consist of a thin layer of gypsum plaster between two sheets of heavy paper. Different thicknesses and kinds of covering on the drywall offer different levels of moisture resistance, fire resistance, and other characteristics. Today, drywall construction is used in most new and renovated buildings because drywall can be installed cheaply and quickly. The panels are easier to work with than traditional plaster, which must be applied wet and allowed to dry before work can proceed. The widespread use of drywall has created a need for workers who are skilled in its installation.

Nature of the Work

Drywall panels are manufactured in standard sizes, such as four feet by twelve feet or four feet by eight feet. With such large sizes, the panels are heavy and awkward to handle and many times must be cut into pieces. The pieces must be fitted together and applied over the entire surface of walls, ceilings, soffits, shafts, and partitions, including any odd-shaped and small areas, like those above or below windows.

Installers begin by measuring the wall or ceiling areas and marking the drywall panels with chalk lines and markers. Using a straightedge and utility knife, they score the board along the cutting lines and break off the excess. With a keyhole saw, they cut openings for electric outlets, vents, air-conditioning units, and plumbing fixtures. Then they fit the pieces into place. They may fasten the pieces directly to the building's inside frame with adhesives, and they secure the drywall permanently with screws or nails.

Often the drywall is attached to a metal framework or a furring grid that the drywall installers put up to support the drywall. When such a framework is to be used, installers must first study blueprints to plan the work procedures and determine what materials, tools, and assistance they will require. They measure, mark, and cut metal runners and studs and bolt them together to make floor-to-ceiling frames. Furring is anchored in the ceiling to form rectangular spaces for ceiling drywall panels. Then the drywall is fitted into place and screwed to the framework.

Because of the weight of drywall, installers are often assisted by helpers. Large ceiling panels may have to be raised with a special lift. After the drywall is in place, drywall installers may measure, cut, assemble, and install prefabricated metal pieces around windows and doors and in other vulnerable places to protect drywall edges. They may also fit and hang doors and install door hardware such as locks, as well as decorative trim around windows, doorways, and vents.

Drywall finishers, or tapers, seal and conceal the joints where drywall panels come together and prepare the walls for painting or papering. Either by hand or with an electric mixer, they prepare a quick-drying sealing material called joint compound, then spread the paste into and over the joints with a special trowel or spatula. While the paste is still wet, the finishers press perforated paper tape over the joint and smooth it to imbed it in the joint compound and cover the joint line. On large commercial projects, this pasting-and-taping operation is accomplished in one step with an automatic applicator. When the sealer is dry, the finishers spread another two coats of cementing material over the tape and blend it into the wall to completely conceal the joint. Any cracks, holes, or imperfections in the walls or ceiling are also filled with joint compound, and nail and screw heads are covered. After a final sanding of the patched areas, the surfaces are ready to be painted or papered. Drywall finishers may apply textured surfaces to walls and ceilings with trowels, brushes, rollers, or spray guns.

Requirements

Most employers prefer applicants who have completed high school, although many hire workers who are not graduates. High school courses in carpentry provide a good background, and mathematics is also important. Drywall workers should be in good physical condition.

Most drywall installers and finishers are trained on the job, beginning as helpers aiding experienced workers. Installer helpers carry materials, hold panels, and clean up. They learn how to measure, cut, and install panels. Finisher helpers tape joints and seal nail holes and scratches. In a short time, they learn to install corner guards and to conceal openings around pipes. After they have become skilled workers, both kinds of helpers complete their training by learning how to estimate the costs of installing and finishing drywall.

Some drywall workers learn the trade through apprenticeship programs, which combine classroom study with on-the-job training. A major union in this field, the United Brotherhood of Carpenters and Joiners of America, offers four-year apprenticeships in carpentry that include instruction in drywall installation. A similar four-year program for nonunion workers is conducted by local affiliates of the Associated Builders and Contractors and the National Association of Home Builders. A two-year apprenticeship for finishers is run by the International Brotherhood of Painters and Allied Trades. Union membership is not a requirement for all drywall workers. Some installers belong to the United Brotherhood of Carpenters and

Joiners of America, and some finishers are members of the International Brotherhood of Painters and Allied Trades.

Opportunities for Experience & Exploration

It may be possible for students to visit a job site and observe installers and finishers at work. Part-time or summer employment as a helper to drywall workers, carpenters, or painters or even as a laborer on a construction job is a good way to get some practical experience in this field.

Methods of Entering

People who want to work in this field can start out as on-the-job trainees or as apprentices. Those who plan to learn the trade as they work may apply directly to contracting companies for entry-level jobs as helpers. Good places to look for job openings include the offices of the state employment service, the classified ads section in local newspapers, and the local offices of the major unions in the field. Information about apprenticeship possibilities may be obtained from local contractors or local unions.

Advancement

Opportunities for advancement are rather good for people who stay in the trade. Experienced workers who show leadership abilities and good judgment may be promoted to be supervisors of work crews. Sometimes they become cost estimators for contractors. Another option is to open your own drywall contracting business.

Employment Outlook

Over the next ten to fifteen years, employment of drywall installers and finishers will increase at about the same rate as the average for all other occupations. Drywall will continue to be used in many kinds of building construction, and it is expected that the level of construction activity will generally remain strong.

Jobs will be located throughout the country, although they will be more plentiful in metropolitan areas, where contractors have enough business to hire full-time drywall workers. In small towns, carpenters often handle drywall installation, and painters may do finishing work. Like other construction trades workers, drywall installers and finishers may go through periods of unemployment or part-time employment when the local economy is in a downturn and construction activity slows.

Earnings

The annual earnings of drywall workers vary widely. The majority of workers have earnings that fall roughly between $20,000 and $40,000, with some making significantly more. Apprentices generally receive about half the rate earned by journeymen workers.

Some drywallers are paid according to the hours they work; the pay of others is based on how much work they complete. For example, a contractor might pay installers and finishers five to six cents for every square foot of panel installed. The average worker is capable of installing thirty-five to forty panels a day, with each panel measuring four feet by twelve feet.

Drywall workers normally work a standard workweek of thirty-five to forty hours. Construction schedules sometimes require installers and finishers to work longer hours or during evenings or on weekends. Workers who are paid by the hour receive extra pay at these times.

Conditions of Work

Drywall installation and finishing can be strenuous work. The large panels are difficult to handle and frequently require more than one person to maneuver them into position. Workers must spend long hours on their feet, often bending and kneeling. To work high up on walls or on ceilings, workers must stand on stilts, ladders, or scaffolding, risking falls unless they use caution. Another possible hazard is injury from power tools, such as saws and nailers. Because sanding creates a lot of dust, finishers wear protective masks and safety glasses.

Drywall installation and finishing is indoor work that can be done in any season of the year. Unlike workers in some construction occupations, drywall workers seldom lose time because of adverse weather conditions.

Sources of Additional Information

■ **International Joint Painting, Decorating, and Drywall Apprenticeship and Manpower Training Fund**
1750 New York Avenue, NW, 8th Floor
Washington, DC 20006
Tel: 202-783-7770

Electricians

School Subjects
Mathematics
Physics

Personal Interests
Computers

Work Environment
Primarily indoors
Primarily multiple locations

Minimum Education Level
High school diploma
Apprenticeship

Salary Range
$15,000 to $50,000

Certification or Licensing
Required for certain positions

Outlook
About as fast as the average

DOT: 003   **GOE:** 05.01.01   **NOC:** 2241

Definition

Electricians design, lay out, assemble, install, test, and repair electrical fixtures, apparatus, and wiring used in a wide range of electrical, telecommunications, and data communications systems that provide light, heat, refrigeration, air conditioning, power, and communications.

History

Electrically powered devices and equipment have fundamentally altered our experience of work, communication, and a multitude of other aspects of daily life. We have so completely adapted to using electrical power that in many ways life without it is hard to imagine. Our dependence on electricity is likely to increase in the future, as new and different machines are perfected to serve human needs. And as long as electric power runs these machines, electricians, the skilled workers who know how to put together and maintain electrical systems, will be in demand nearly everywhere.

It was during the latter part of the nineteenth century that electric power entered everyday life. Before then, electricity was the subject of experimentation and theorizing, but few practical applications. The widespread use of electricity was spurred by a combination of innovations, especially the discovery of a way to transmit power efficiently via overhead lines and the invention of the incandescent lamp, the telephone, and the electric telegraph. In the 1880s, commercial supplies of electricity began to be available in some cities, and within a few years electric power was transforming many homes and factories.

Early electrical workers were mainly concerned with setting up the lines and supporting poles for distributing power around cities. The work of these pioneers, who were often called *linemen,* was difficult and dangerous, and serious accidents were common. As electrical distribution systems grew larger and more complicated and wiring was extended into many buildings, linemen developed new tools and techniques for safely installing circuits and equipment. *Wiremen,* specialists in wiring buildings, emerged as a distinct group of essential craft workers in the building and construction trades.

Today, electricians are the workers who perform such tasks. Along with the electricians who install and repair electrical systems for buildings, the field includes people who work on a wide array of telecommunications equipment, industrial machine-tool controls, marine facilities like ships and off-shore drilling rigs, and many other kinds of sophisticated equipment that have been developed using twentieth-century technology. In all of these applications, electricians are responsible for establishing and maintaining vital links between power-generating plants and the many electrical and electronic systems that shape our lives.

Nature of the Work

Many electricians specialize in either construction or maintenance work, although some work in both fields. Electricians in construction are usually employed by electrical contractors. Other construction electricians work for building contractors or for industrial plants, public utilities, state highway commissions, or other large organizations that employ workers directly to build or remodel their property. A few are self-employed.

Maintenance electricians, also known as *electrical repairers,* may work in large factories, office buildings, small plants, or wherever existing electrical facilities and machinery need regular servicing to keep them in good working order. Many maintenance electricians work in manufacturing industries, such as those that produce automobiles, aircraft, ships, steel, chemicals, and industrial machinery. Some are employed by hospitals, municipalities, housing complexes, or shopping centers to do maintenance, repair, and sometimes installation work. Some work for or operate businesses that contract to repair and update wiring in residences and commercial buildings.

When installing electrical systems, electricians may follow blueprints and specifications, or they may be told verbally what is needed. They may prepare sketches showing the intended location of wiring and equipment. Once the plan is clear, they measure, cut, assemble, and install plastic-covered wire or electrical conduit, which is a tube or channel through which heavier grades of electrical wire or cable are run. They strip insulation from wires, splice and solder wires together, and tape or cap the ends. They attach cables and wiring to the incoming electrical service and to various fixtures and machines that use electricity. They install switches, circuit breakers, relays, transformers, grounding leads, signal devices, and other electrical components. After the installation is complete, they test circuits for continuity and safety, adjusting the setup as needed.

Electricians must work according to the National Electric Code and state and local building and electrical codes (electrical codes are standards that electrical systems must meet to ensure safe, reliable functioning). In doing their work, electricians should always try to use materials efficiently, plan for future access to the area for service and maintenance on the system, and avoid hazardous and unsightly wiring arrangements, making their work as neat and orderly as possible.

Electricians use a variety of equipment ranging from simple hand tools such as screwdrivers, pliers, wrenches, and hacksaws to power tools such as drills, hydraulic benders for metal conduit, and electric soldering guns and also testing devices such as oscilloscopes, ammeters, and test lamps. *Construction electricians* often supply their own hand tools. Experienced workers may have hundreds of dollars invested in tools.

Maintenance electricians do many of the same kinds of tasks, but their activities are usually aimed at preventing trouble before it occurs. They periodically inspect equipment and carry out routine service procedures, often according to a predetermined schedule. They repair or replace worn or defective parts and keep management informed about the reliability of the electrical systems. If any breakdowns occur, maintenance electricians must return the equipment to full functioning as soon as possible so that the expense and inconvenience are minimal.

A growing number of electricians are involved in activities other than constructing and maintaining electrical systems in buildings.

Many are employed to install computer wiring and equipment, telephone wiring, or the coaxial and fiber optics cables used in telecommunications and computer equipment. Electricians also work in power plants, where electric power is generated; in machine shops, where electric motors are repaired and rebuilt; aboard ships, fixing communications and navigation systems; at locations that need large lighting and power installations, such as airports and mines; and in numerous other settings.

Requirements

Some electricians still learn their trade the same way electrical workers did many years ago—informally on the job, while employed as helpers to skilled workers. Especially if that experience is supplemented with vocational or technical school courses, correspondence courses, or training received in the military, electrical helpers may in time become well-qualified craft workers in some area of the field.

However, it is generally accepted that apprenticeship programs provide the best all-around training in this trade. Apprenticeships combine a series of planned, structured, supervised job experiences with classroom instruction in related subjects. Many programs are designed to give apprentices a variety of experiences by having them work for several electrical contractors doing different kinds of jobs. Typically, apprenticeships last four to five years. Completion of an apprenticeship is usually a significant advantage in getting the better jobs in the field.

Applicants for apprenticeships generally need to be high school graduates, at least eighteen years of age, in good health, and with at least average physical strength. Although local requirements vary, many applicants are required to take tests to determine their aptitude for the work.

All prospective electricians, whether they intend to enter an apprenticeship or learn informally on the job, ought to have a high school background that includes such courses as applied mathematics and science, shop classes that teach the use of various tools, and mechanical drawing. Electronics courses are especially important for those who plan to become maintenance electricians. Good color vision is necessary, because electricians need to be able to distinguish color-coded wires. Agility and manual dexterity are also desirable characteristics.

Most apprenticeship programs are developed and conducted by state and national contractor associations such as the Independent Electrical Contractors, Inc. and the union locals of the International Brotherhood of Electrical Workers. Some programs are conducted as cooperative efforts between such groups and local community colleges and training organizations. In either situation, the apprenticeship program is usually managed by a training committee. An agreement regarding in-class and on-the-job training is usually established between the committee and each apprentice.

Usually apprenticeships involve at least 144 hours of classroom work each year, covering such subjects as electrical theory, electronics, blueprint reading, mathematics, electrical code requirements, and first aid. On the job, apprentices learn how to safely use and care for tools, equipment, and materials commonly encountered in the trade. Over the years of the program, they spend about 8,000 hours working under the supervision of experienced electricians. They begin with simple tasks, such as drilling holes and setting up conduit. As they acquire skills and knowledge, they progress to more difficult tasks, like diagramming electrical systems and connecting and testing wiring and electrical components.

Many electricians find that after they are working in the field, they still need to take courses to keep abreast of new developments. Unions and employers may sponsor classes introducing new methods and materials or explaining changes in electrical code requirements. By taking skill-improvement courses electricians may also improve their chances for advancement to better-paying positions.

Electricians may or may not belong to a union. While many electricians belong to such organizations as the International Brotherhood of Electrical Workers; the International Union of Electronic, Electrical, Salaried, Machine, and Furniture Workers; the International Association of Machinists and Aerospace Workers; and other unions, an increasing number of electricians are opting to affiliate with independent (nonunion) electrical contractors.

Some states and municipalities require that electricians be licensed. To obtain a license, electricians usually must pass a written examination on electrical theory, National Electrical Code requirements, and local building and electrical codes.

Opportunities for Experience & Exploration

High school students can get an idea about their aptitude for and interest in tasks that come up regularly in the work of electricians by taking such courses as metal and electrical shop, drafting, electronics, and mathematics. Hobbies like repairing radios, building electronics kits, or working with model electric trains involve skills similar to those needed by electricians. In addition to sampling related activities like these, prospective electricians may benefit by arranging to talk with an electrician about his or her job. Perhaps with the help of a teacher or guidance counselor, it may be possible to contact a local electrical contracting firm and locate someone willing to give an insider's description of the occupation.

Methods of Entering

People seeking to enter this field may either begin working as helpers with little background in the field or they may enter an apprenticeship program. Leads for helper jobs may be located by contacting electrical contractors directly and by checking the usual sources for jobs listings, such as the local offices of the state employment service and newspaper classified advertising sections. Students in trade and vocational school courses may be able to find job openings through the placement office of their school.

People who want to become apprentices may start by contacting the union local of the International Brotherhood of Electrical Workers, the local chapter of the Independent Electrical Contractors, Inc., or the local apprenticeship training committee. Information on apprenticeship possibilities can also be obtained through the state employment service.

Advancement

The advancement possibilities for skilled, experienced electricians depend partly on their field of activity. Those who work in construction may become supervisors, job site superintendents, or estimators for electrical contractors. Some electricians are able to establish their own contracting businesses, although in many areas contractors must obtain a special license. Another possibility for some electricians is to move, for example, from construction to maintenance work or into jobs in the shipbuilding, automobile, or aircraft industry.

Employment Outlook

During the next ten to fifteen years, job opportunities for skilled electricians are expected to be good, although the Bureau of Labor Statistics is predicting slower than average growth for electricians as a whole. The growth in this field will be principally related to overall increased levels in construction of buildings for residential and commercial purposes. In addition, growth will be driven by our ever-increasing use of electrical and electronic devices and equipment. Electricians will be called on to upgrade old wiring and to install and maintain more extensive wiring systems than has been necessary in the past. In particular, the increased use of sophisticated telecommunications and data-processing equipment and automated manufacturing systems is expected to lead to many job opportunities for electricians.

While the overall outlook for this occupational field is good, the availability of jobs will vary over time and from place to place. In construction, the amount of activity goes up and down depending on the state of the local and national economy. Thus, during economic slowdowns, opportunities for construction electricians may not be plentiful. People working in this field need to be prepared for periods of unemployment between construction projects. Openings for apprentices also decline during economic downturns. Maintenance electricians are usually less vulnerable to periodic unemployment because they are more likely to work for one employer that needs electrical services on a steady basis. But if they work in an industry where the economy causes big fluctuations in the level of activity, such as automobile manufacturing, they may be laid off during recessions.

Not many electricians switch completely out of their job field, because of the time that must be invested in training and the relatively good pay for skilled workers. Nonetheless, many of the job openings that occur each year develop as electricians move into other occupations or leave the labor force altogether. During the coming years, enough electricians are expected to retire that a national shortage of well-qualified workers could develop if training programs don't attract more applicants who can eventually take the place of the retirees.

Earnings

The earnings of electricians vary widely depending on such factors as the industry in which they are employed, their geographic location, union membership, and other factors. In general, the majority of electricians who are employed full time have annual earnings in the range of $21,000 to $37,000 or more. One national survey has showed that the average wages for electricians who are union members are at least $33,700 a year. Another study has showed that maintenance electricians in metropolitan areas have earnings that average at least around $34,000 a year. Electricians in the West and Midwest tend to make more than those in the Northeast and South.

Wage rates for many electricians are set by agreements between unions and employers. In addition to their regular earnings, electricians may receive fringe benefits such as employer contributions to health insurance and pension plans, paid vacation and sick days, and supplemental unemployment compensation plans.

Wages of apprentices often start at about 40 to 50 percent of the skilled worker's rate and increase every six months until the last period of the apprenticeship, when the pay approaches that of fully qualified electricians.

Conditions of Work

Electricians usually work indoors, although some must do tasks outdoors or in buildings that are still under construction. The standard workweek is about forty hours. In many jobs overtime may be required. Maintenance electricians often have to work some weekend, holiday, or night hours because they must service equipment that operates all the time.

Electricians often spend long periods on their feet, sometimes on ladders or scaffolds or in awkward or uncomfortable places. The work is sometimes strenuous. Electricians may have to put up with noise and dirt on the job. They may risk injuries such as falls off ladders, electrical shocks, and cuts and bruises. By following established safety practices, most of these hazards can be avoided.

Sources of Additional Information

For a general brochure on electrical apprenticeship, contact:

■ **National Joint Apprenticeship Training Committee for the Electrical Industry**
16201 Trade Zone Avenue, Suite 105
Upper Marlboro, MD 20774

For information on its electrical apprenticeship curriculum and a list of chapter offices, contact:

■ **Independent Electrical Contractors, Inc.**
507 Wythe Street
Alexandria, VA 22314
Tel: 703-549-7351

Electricians

For a list of local unions in your area, contact:

■ **International Brotherhood of Electrical Workers**
1125 15th Street, NW
Washington, DC 20005

■ **National Electrical Contractors Association**
3 Bethesda Metro Center, Suite 1100
Bethesda, MD 20814

■ **International Society of Certified Electronics Technicians**
2708 West Berry Street
Fort Worth, TX 76109

Elevator Installers and Repairers

School Subjects
Mathematics
Shop

Personal Interests
Figuring out how things work
Fixing things

Work Environment
Primarily indoors
Primarily multiple locations

Minimum Education Level
High school diploma
Apprenticeship

Salary Range
$20,000 to $56,000+

Certification or Licensing
Required

Outlook
As fast as the average

DOT: 825   **GOE:** 05.05.06   **NOC:** 7318

Definition

Elevator installers and repairers, also called *elevator constructors* or *elevator mechanics,* are skilled craft workers who assemble, install, and repair elevators, escalators, dumbwaiters, and similar equipment.

History

The use of mechanical devices for lifting loads dates back at least to the time of the ancient Romans, who used platforms attached to pulleys in constructing buildings. In the seventeenth century, a crude passenger elevator known as the "flying chair" was invented. These early elevators were operated by human, animal, or water power.

By the early nineteenth century, steam was used to power machines that raised elevators. For about the first half of the century, elevators were almost always used for lifting freight. This was because the hemp ropes that hauled the elevators were not strong enough to be safe for passenger use. In 1852, Elisha G. Otis designed and installed the first elevator with a safety device that prevented it from falling if the rope broke. Five years later, Otis's first safety elevator for carrying passengers was put into use in a store in New York City, and it was immediately declared a success.

Steam-powered elevators were used until the 1880s, when elevators powered by electricity were introduced. Subsequent design changes brought a series of improvements such as push-button operation; taller shafts and faster speeds, so that the elevators could be used even in skyscrapers; and power doors and automatic operation, which made elevators more economical than they had been when human operators were necessary. Today's elevators are often electronically controlled and may be capable of moving up and down at two thousand feet per minute.

The escalator, or moving stairway, was invented in 1891 by Jesse W. Reno. Early escalators, like modern ones, were electrically powered and resembled an inclined endless belt held in position by two tracks. Moving sidewalks and ramps are based on the same principle, but they are level or inclined at much lower angles than escalators. Today it is rare to find a newer commercial, industrial, or apartment building that is not equipped with elevators for passengers or freight, and perhaps escalators as well.

Almost as long as these machines have been in use in buildings to move people and their belongings, there has been a need for workers who specialize in assembling, installing, and maintaining them. There are presently more than twenty-five thousand workers in this field, and the majority are employed by contractors specializing in the elevator field.

Nature of the Work

Elevator installers and repairers may service and update old equipment that has been in operation for many years or they may work on new systems, which may be equipped with state-of-the-art microprocessors capable of monitoring a whole elevator system and automatically operating it with maximum possible efficiency. Installing and repairing modern elevators requires a good understanding of electricity, electronics, and hydraulics.

Installers begin their work by examining plans and blueprints that describe the equipment to be installed. They need to determine the layout of the components, including the framework, guide rails, motors, pumps, cylinders, plunger foundations, and electrical connections. Once the layout is clear, they install the guide rails (for guiding the elevator as it moves up and down) on the walls of the shaft. Then they run electrical wiring in the shaft between floors and install controls and other devices on each floor and at a central control panel. They assemble the parts of the car at the bottom of the shaft. They bolt or weld together the steel frame and attach walls, doors, and parts that keep the car from moving from side to side as it travels up and down the shaft. They also install the entrance doors and door frames on each floor.

Installers also set up and connect the equipment that moves the cars. In cable elevator systems, steel cables are attached to each car and, at their other end, to a large counterweight. Hoisting machinery, often located at the top of the shaft, moves the cables around a pulley, thus moving the elevator car up or down and the counterweight in the opposite direction. In hydraulic systems, the car rests on a hydraulic cylinder that is raised and lowered by a pump, thus moving the elevator car up and down like an automobile on a lift. After the various parts of the elevator system are in place, the elevator installers test the operation of the system and make any necessary adjustments so that the installation meets building and safety code requirements.

In hotels, restaurants, hospitals, and other institutions where food is prepared, elevator installers may work on dumbwaiters, which are small elevators for transporting food and dishes from one part of a building to another. They may also work on escalators, installing wiring, motors, controls, the stairs, the framework for the stairs, and the tracks that keep the stairs in position.

After elevator and escalator equipment is installed, it needs regular adjustment and maintenance services to ensure that the system continues to function in a safe, reliable manner. Elevator repairers routinely inspect the equipment, perform safety tests using meters and gauges, clean parts that are prone to getting dirty, make adjustments, replace worn components, and lubricate bearings and other moving parts.

Repairers also do minor emergency repairs, such as replacing defective parts. Finding the cause of malfunctions often involves troubleshooting. For this reason, repairers need a strong mechanical aptitude. In addition, repairers may work as part of crews that do major repair and modernization work on older equipment.

Elevator installers and repairers use a variety of hand tools, power tools, welding equipment, and electrical testing devices such as digital multimeters, logic probes, and oscilloscopes.

Requirements

Employers prefer to hire high school graduates who are at least eighteen years of age and in good physical condition. Mechanical aptitude, an interest in machines, and some technical training related to the field are other important qualifications. High school or vocational school courses that would be good background for this field include mathematics, machine shop, applied physics, electronics, and blueprint reading.

Union elevator installers and repairers receive their training through the National Elevator Industry Educational Program, administered on a local level by committees made up of local employers who belong to the National Elevator Industry, and local branches of the International Union of Elevator Constructors. The program consists of on-the-job training under the supervision of experienced workers, together with classroom instruction in related subjects. In the work portion of the program, trainees begin by doing the simplest tasks and gradually progress to more difficult activities. In the classroom they learn about installation procedures, basic electrical theory, electronics, and job safety.

Union trainees spend their first six months in the industry in a probationary status. Those who complete the period successfully go on to become elevator constructor helpers. After successfully completing four years of required field and classroom education, they become eligible to take a validated mechanic exam. Upon passing this exam, workers become fully qualified installers and repairers. They may be able to advance more quickly if they already have a good technical background, acquired by taking courses at a postsecondary technical school or junior college.

Because the technology used in elevator systems is constantly changing, even well-trained and experienced elevator installers and repairers may periodically have to upgrade their skills by attending courses that introduce new equipment and techniques or by taking correspondence courses.

Although, union membership is not necessarily a requirement for employment, most elevator installers and repairers are members of the International Union of Elevator Constructors. Additionally, most states and municipalities require that elevator installers and repairers pass a licensing examination.

Opportunities for Experience & Exploration

High school courses such as electrical shop, machine shop, and blueprint reading can give students a hands-on sense of tasks that are similar to everyday activities of elevator installers and repairers. A part-time or summer job as a helper at a commercial building site may provide an opportunity to observe the conditions that these workers encounter on the job. If it can be arranged, a visit to an elevator manufacturing firm can be informative. It also may be possible to learn about working in this field by talking to someone recommended by local representatives of the International Union of Elevator Constructors.

Methods of Entering

People seeking information about trainee positions in this field should try contacting contractors who specialize in elevator maintenance and repair work, the local office of the International Union of Elevator Constructors, or elevator manufacturers. The local office of the state employment service may also be a source of information and job leads.

Advancement

When they have completed their approximately four-year training program, met any local licensure requirements, and successfully passed a validated mechanic exam, workers in this field are considered fully qualified. With further experience, those who work for elevator contracting firms may become eligible for promotion to positions such as mechanics-in-charge or supervisors, coordinating the work done by other installers. Or they may become estimators, figuring the costs for supplies and labor for work before it is done. Working for an elevator manufacturer, they may move into sales positions, jobs related to product design, and management. Other experienced workers become inspectors employed by the government to check elevators and escalators to make sure that they comply with specifications and safety codes.

Employment Outlook

Over the next ten to fifteen years, employment of elevator installers and repairers is likely to increase at about the same rate as the average for other occupations. The demand for these workers will be related to the level of building construction activity and to the need to modernize old elevator installations. But even during economic downturns, installers and repairers will be needed to do maintenance work and to put in replacement equipment from minor components to large portions of elevator systems.

Most new job openings will occur when workers change to new occupations or leave the labor force altogether. As the technology in the industry becomes more complex, employers will increasingly seek workers who are technically well trained.

Earnings

Earnings depend on a variety of factors such as experience and geographical location. Overall, the average annual earnings of elevator installers and repairers are in the range of $37,000. Mechanics-in-charge may have earnings over $56,000 a year. Probationary workers start at about 50 percent of the full wage; after the initial period, trainees earn about 70 percent of the full wage. In addition to regular wages, union elevator installers and repairers receive other benefits including health insurance, pension plans, paid holidays and vacations, and some tuition-free courses in subjects related to their work.

Conditions of Work

The standard workweek for elevator installers and repairers is forty hours. Some workers put in overtime hours (for which they are paid extra), and some repairers are on call for responding to emergencies for twenty-four-hour periods.

Most repair work is done indoors, so little time is lost because of bad weather. It is frequently necessary to lift heavy equipment and parts and to work in very hot or cold, cramped, or awkward places.

Sources of Additional Information

- **International Union of Elevator Constructors**
  5565 Sterret Place, Suite 310
  Columbia, MD 21044
  Tel: 410-997-9000

- **National Elevator and Escalator Association**
  #708, 6299 Airport Road
  Mississauga, ON L4V 1N3 Canada
  Tel: 905-678-9940

- **National Elevator Industry Educational Program**
  11 Larsen Way
  Attleboro Falls, MA 02763
  Tel: 508-699-2200

Floor Covering Installers

School Subjects
Mathematics
Shop (Trade/Vo-tech education)

Personal Interests
Fixing things
Model building

Work Environment
Primarily indoors
Primarily multiple locations

Minimum Education Level
High school diploma
Apprenticeship

Salary Range
$25,000 to $45,000+

Certification or Licensing
None

Outlook
About as fast as the average

DOT: 864   **GOE:** 05.10.01   **NOC:** 7295

Definition

Floor covering installers include *resilient floor layers,* who install, replace, and repair shock-absorbing, sound-deadening, or decorative floor covering such as vinyl tile and sheet vinyl on finished interior floors of buildings, and *carpet layers,* who install carpets and rugs, especially wall-to-wall carpeting.

History

Around 1840, Erastus Bigelow, an American industrialist, developed a power carpet loom, the first in a series that revolutionized carpet manufacturing. The looms that Bigelow invented made possible the production of large quantities of attractive carpeting at reasonable prices and helped open the way for wide acceptance of machine-made wall-to-wall carpeting as a standard covering for floors in middle-class homes and businesses.

Another flooring first made during that era was linoleum. Patented in 1863, it was an inexpensive, durable, resilient flooring made of a composition of linseed oil, powdered cork, and other ingredients on a fiber backing. An early kind of linoleum, called battleship linoleum, was first used on the decks of warships.

Many floor coverings today are made of materials that have been developed since World War II. The synthetic fibers now in carpets frequently have significant practical advantages over the natural fibers used many years ago. Over the years, various materials have been used in resilient flooring, including rubber, asphalt, and cork. Linoleum is no longer manufactured in the United States, although linoleum floors still exist, particularly in older buildings. Newer resilient flooring is most often made of vinyl, a synthetic plastic material.

With the popularity of flooring materials like these came the need for skilled workers who could efficiently measure, cut, and install the materials so that they fit exactly, stayed in place, and presented a good appearance. Today floor covering installation is a well-established craft in the building trades.

Nature of the Work

Installers' tasks vary somewhat according to whether they specialize in the installation of carpets or resilient floor coverings. Some installers do both types of coverings.

For both types of flooring, the preparation of the surface beneath the finish material is very important. The subfloor surface must be firm, dry, smooth, and free of loose dust and dirt. Installers may have to sweep, scrape, sand, or chip dirt and other irregularities from the floor, as well as fill cracks with a filler material. Sometimes a new surface of plywood or cement must be laid down before any floor covering can be installed.

Experienced installers must be able to gauge the moisture content of the subfloor and decide whether conditions are suitable for installing the covering. They should also know about the various adhesives that can be used, depending on conditions. Once the subfloor surface is prepared, installers consult blueprints or sketches and carefully measure the floor to determine where joints and seams will fall.

When the layout is clear, the installers, perhaps assisted by apprentices or helpers, measure and cut the floor covering to create sections of the proper size. They use a rule, straightedge, linoleum knife, and snips. They may also cut and lay in place on the subfloor a foundation material such as felt. Then they apply adhesive cement to the floor and cement the foundation in place. With chalk lines and dividers, installers lay out lines on the foundation material to guide them in installing the floor covering. They trowel on adhesive cement and lay the floor covering in place, following the guidelines. Installers must be especially careful to align the pieces if there is any pattern in the flooring. They must also pay particular attention to fitting the pieces in odd-shaped areas around door openings, pipes, and posts. To make tight seams where sections of sheet covering must join, they overlap edges and cut through both layers with a knife. After the covering is laid in place, they often run a roller over it to smooth it and ensure good adhesion.

In installing wall-to-wall carpeting, carpet layers first measure the floor and plan the layout. They should allow for expected foot-traffic patterns so that the best appearance and longest wear will be obtained from the carpet. They also must locate seams where they will be least noticed.

When the layout is completed, installers make sure that the floor surface is in the proper condition and correct any imperfections that may show through the carpet. Some carpet can be tacked directly to certain kinds of floor, but in many buildings, including residences, installers often use the tackless strip method of laying carpet. A tackless strip is a thin strip of plywood with rows of steel pins projecting upward from it to grip carpeting firmly in place. Installers nail tackless strips around the border of the floor. Next, they cut and place padding in the open area of the floor.

Carpet often comes in twelve-foot widths, so some rooms require that sections of carpet be seamed together. If the carpet has not been precut and seamed in the floor covering firm's workroom, the installers must use a carpet knife to cut pieces to the correct sizes, then attach the pieces together. They may sew the seam with a curved needle or use a heat-activated adhesive tape and an electric heating tool like an iron.

When pieces are cut and ready, the installers position the carpet and stretch it with special tools so it fits evenly on the floor, with no lumps or rolls. They fasten it in place, either with the tackless strips or by tacking directly to the floor. Any excess material must be trimmed off so that the carpet meets the wall and door thresholds with a snug, exact fit.

Carpet installers use hand tools, including mallets, staple guns, pry bars, trowels, carpet knives, and shears; measuring and marking devices, such as tape measures, straightedges, and chalk lines; and power tools, such as stretchers.

Requirements

Floor covering installers can learn their skills on the job or through apprenticeship programs, which combine on-the-job training with classroom instruction.

Most installers begin as helpers working for flooring installation contractors and learn informally on the job. When they are first hired, helpers are assigned simple tasks, such as tacking down strips. As they gain skills and experience, they are given more difficult work, such as measuring and cutting. Employers look for applicants who have manual dexterity and good eye-hand coordination. They may require that helpers have a high school education. High school courses that are good background for applicants include wood and metal shop classes, mechanical drawing, general mathematics, and geometry. Because installers work on the premises of the customer, they should have a neat appearance and a courteous manner. It may take an installer eighteen months to two years of informal on-the-job training to learn the basics of carpet laying or resilient floor laying.

Apprenticeship programs, which often last three to four years, usually provide much more complete training in all phases of installation. Some apprenticeships teach installation of both types of flooring, while others teach one or the other. Apprentices work under the supervision of experienced installers and typically attend classes in related subjects once a week.

Opportunities for Experience & Exploration

High school shop courses can introduce students to the hand tools and skills that floor covering installers use, and courses in applied mathematics can help students gauge their ability to do the kinds of computations that installers must do. A part-time or summer job as a helper working for a flooring installation contractor would be a good way to directly experience this work and might lead to full-time employment later. Even a do-it-yourself home improvement project installing vinyl floor tiles can provide a sample of the activities of these workers.

Methods of Entering

People who plan to start out as helpers in this field and learn their skills on the job can apply directly to floor covering contractors and retailers. For specific job leads, they may want to check the listings in newspaper classified ads or the local offices of the state employment service. Information on apprenticeships in the area may be available from contractors, the state employment service, or the local offices of unions to which some installers belong, such as the United Brotherhood of Carpenters and Joiners of America and the International Brotherhood of Painters and Allied Trades.

Advancement

Installers who work for large floor-laying firms may be promoted to positions in which they supervise crews of installers. Installers who are familiar with the business, get along well with people, and can communicate effectively may move into sales jobs with retailers of flooring products. Or they may become estimators, workers who measure floors, compute areas, and figure costs using their knowledge of the materials and labor required for various kinds of installations.

With additional education and training, installers may go to work for manufacturers of floor covering materials, becoming, for example, manufacturers' representatives to retailers. Many installers decide to go into business for themselves as independent subcontractors.

Employment Outlook

In the 1990s, there are more than 115,000 floor covering installers employed in the United States, including about 73,000 who work mainly or exclusively with carpets. Over the next ten to fifteen years, employment of these workers is expected to increase at a rate that is close to the average for all occupations. Installers will be needed to put down flooring in newly constructed buildings and to replace flooring in older buildings that are being refurbished. Even during economic downturns, when new construction levels drop drastically, the need to renovate existing buildings will mean some employment opportunities will continue to be available for installers.

During coming years, most job opportunities that open up will probably occur when experienced workers leave the field for other occupations, retire, or die.

Carpeting continues to be a very popular floor covering, a sign that the demand for carpet installers will continue. Carpet can easily be installed on the plywood and concrete floors that are common in new buildings today. Modern carpet fibers, which are long-wearing, stain-resistant, and come in many colors and styles, are making carpeting increasingly attractive as a choice of floor covering.

Earnings

The earnings of floor covering installers vary depending on their geographic location, whether their wages are set by union contracts, and other factors. Installers in the West tend to be paid more than the national average, while those in the South make less than the average. Overall, experienced workers have earnings that average roughly $25,000 a year. The median earnings of carpet layers are apparently somewhat lower. A few workers can make more than $45,000 a year. Starting wages for apprentices and other trainees are usually about one-half the rate for experienced workers.

Most installers are paid by the hour, but some are paid by the number of yards of flooring they install, a system that can benefit installers who are particularly fast workers.

Conditions of Work

Although installers usually work in the daytime, some flooring replacement work is done at night or on weekends to minimize disruption of offices and stores during business hours. The standard workweek is about forty hours. Installers usually receive overtime for weekend and holiday work. Self-employed installers may work very irregular hours.

Unlike most other construction trades, floor covering installation involves few hazards. The areas where installers work are usually indoors, well lighted, clean, and comfortable. Installers must bend, reach, and stretch often as they work. They sometimes get knee and back injuries, because they must constantly kneel as they work and they lift heavy rolls of floor covering.

Sources of Additional Information

- **Carpet and Rug Institute**
  PO Box 2048
  Dalton, GA 30722
  Tel: 706-278-3178

- **Floor Covering Installation Contractors Association**
  PO Box 948
  Dalton, GA 30722-0948
  Tel: 706-226-5488

- **Resilient Floor Covering Institute**
  966 Hungerford Drive, Suite 12-B
  Rockville, MD 20850
  Tel: 301-340-8580

Glaziers

School Subjects
Mathematics
Shop (Trade/Vo-tech education)

Personal Interests
Cars
Model building

Work Environment
Primarily indoors
Primarily multiple locations

Minimum Education Level
High school diploma
Apprenticeship

Salary Range
$20,000 to $40,000

Certification or Licensing
None

Outlook
About as fast as the average

DOT: 865   **GOE:** 05.10.01   **NOC:** 7292

Definition

Glaziers select, cut, fit, and install all types of glass and glass substitutes such as plastics. They may install windows, mirrors, shower doors, glass tabletops, display cases, skylights, special items such as preassembled stained glass and leaded glass window panels, and many other glass items.

History

Glass was used in windows at least as early as Roman times, although no installed glass survives from that era. The earliest glass that is still in the windows where it was installed dates back to the twelfth century, when brilliant stained glass windows began to be used in churches and cathedrals in Europe. One reason stained glass became popular was that clear glass suitable for windows was extremely difficult to make. By the fourteenth century, stained glass windows were declining as an art form. Relatively few stained glass windows were made until a revival of the art in the nineteenth century.

From the fourteenth century, handmade crown glass was in demand for windowpanes because of its relative clearness and good quality. Crown glass, which had a center like a bull's eye surrounded by concentric ripple lines, was made by first blowing a gob of molten glass into a pear shape, then flattening it while it was still hot. Beginning in the seventeenth century, crown glass was gradually replaced as a window glass by glass manufactured using other processes. During the colonial era in the United States, however, there was great demand for crown glass, which was produced in Boston from 1793 to about 1827.

Compared to its use today, there was very little glass used in buildings until the nineteenth century. But a flood of manufacturing innovations revolutionized glassmaking, and by the mid-1800s the output of clear flat glass was vastly increased. Glass became popular in many new applications in buildings. Along with the increased demand for glass was a new demand for trained glaziers to cut and install glass. In the twentieth century, the continuing development of new kinds of glass, new manufacturing processes, and new methods of cutting, joining, and sealing glass in place assures glaziers that they will be providing important services in the construction industry for many years to come.

Nature of the Work

Glaziers install different kinds of glass in different places. They put insulating glass where it is desirable to keep heat or sound on one side and laminated glass in doors and windows where safety is a concern. They install large structural glass panels on building exteriors to create walls that admit natural light. They install mirrors, storefronts, automobile windows, and sun-space additions to homes.

In most of these applications, the glass is precut to size in a shop or factory and comes to the work site mounted in a frame. Because glass is heavy and easily breakable, glaziers may need to use a hoist or a crane to move large pieces into position. The glass is held with suction cups and gently guided into place.

When it is in place, glaziers often put the glass on a bed of putty or another kind of cement inside a metal or wooden frame and secure the glass with metal clips, metal or wooden molding, bolts, or other devices. They may put a rubber gasket around the outside edges to clamp the glass in place and make a moisture-proof seal. In windows, glaziers may pack a putty-like glazing compound into the joints at the edges of the glass in the molding that surrounds the open space. They trim off the excess compound with a glazing knife to make a neat appearance.

Sometimes glaziers must manually cut glass to size at a work site. They put uncut glass on a rack or cutting table and measure and mark the cutting line. They use a cutting tool like a small, sharp wheel of hard metal, which cuts the glass when rolled firmly over the surface. After making a cut, they break off the excess by hand or with a notched tool.

In some situations, glaziers cut and fasten together pieces of metal. When installing storefront windows, for example, they cut the drain moldings and face moldings that fit around the opening. They screw the drain molding into position and place plate glass into position against the metal. Then they bolt the face molding around the edges and attach metal corner pieces. When installing glass doors, they fit hinges and bolt on handles, locks, and other hardware.

Some workers in glazing occupations specialize in other kinds of glass installations. Among these workers are *aircraft safety glass installers,* who cut and install laminated safety glass in airplane windows and windshields; *auto glass installers,* who replace pitted or broken windows and windshields in motor vehicles; *refrigerator glaziers,* who install the plate glass windows in refrigerator display cases and walk-in coolers; and *glass installers,* who work in planing mills where they fit glass into newly manufactured millwork products, such as doors, window sashes, china cabinets, and office partitions.

Requirements

The best way for glaziers to learn their trade is by completing an apprenticeship program. Apprenticeships last three to four years and combine on-the-job training with classroom instruction in related subjects. Apprenticeship programs are operated by the National Glass Association in cooperation with local committees representing unions and employers or local contractor groups.

Apprentices spend roughly 6,000 hours working under the supervision of experienced glaziers in planned programs that teach all aspects of the trade. Apprentices learn how to use tools and equipment; how to handle, measure, cut, and install glass, molding, and metal framing; and how to install glass doors. Their formal classroom instruction, about 144 hours each year of the apprenticeship, covers subjects such as glass manufacturing, selecting glass for specific purposes, estimating procedures, mathematics, blueprint reading, construction techniques, safety practices, and first aid.

Requirements for admission to apprenticeship programs are set by the local administrators of each program. Typically, applicants need to be high school graduates, at least seventeen years old, in good physical condition, with proven mechanical aptitude. Some previous high school or vocational school courses in applied mathematics, shop, blueprint reading, and similar subjects are desirable as preparation for work in glazing occupations.

Many glaziers also learn their skills informally on the job. They are hired in helper positions and gradually pick up skills as they assist experienced workers. When they start, they are assigned simple tasks, such as carrying glass; later they may get the opportunity to cut glass and do other more complex tasks. Glaziers who learn informally on the job often do not receive as thorough training as apprentices, and the training usually takes longer.

While union membership is not necessarily a requirement for employment, many glaziers who work in construction are members of the International Brotherhood of Painters and Allied Trades.

Opportunities for Experience & Exploration

Prospective glaziers can get an indication of their abilities and interest in similar skilled activities by taking shop courses, blueprint reading, mechanical drawing, and mathematics. Hobbies that require manual dexterity, using a variety of hand tools, and attention to detail are also good experience. Working with stained glass, making decorative objects such as windowpanes, lampshades, and ornaments, is an excellent hobby for the prospective glazier.

For a more direct look at this career, students may be able to get a part-time or summer job as a helper at a construction site or in a glass shop. If this cannot be arranged, it may be possible instead to talk with someone employed in a glass shop or as a glazier in construction work to get an insider's view of the field.

Methods of Entering

People who would like to enter this field either as apprentices or as on-the-job trainees can get more information about local opportunities by contacting area glazing contractors, the local offices of the state employment service, or local offices of the International Brotherhood of Painters and Allied Trades. Information about apprenticeships may also be available through the state apprenticeship agency. Job leads for helper positions may also be listed in newspaper classified ads.

Advancement

Experienced glaziers usually have only a few possible avenues for advancement. In some situations, they can move into supervisory positions, directing the work done by other glazing workers at construction sites or in shops or factories. Or they can become estimators, figuring the costs for labor and materials before jobs are done. Advancement for glaziers often consists of pay increases without changes in job activity.

Employment Outlook

Over the next ten to fifteen years, employment in this occupational field is expected to increase at a rate that is about the same as the average for all occupations. During this period, there will probably be an overall increase in the construction of new buildings that involve substantial glazing, as well as a growing need to update older buildings. Glass will probably continue to be popular for both its good looks and its practical advantages, and further improvements in glass and glass products may well make glass still more desirable as a construction material.

Nonetheless, glaziers who work in construction should realize that there will be variations from time to time and place to place in the opportunities available to them. They should expect to go through periods of unemployment, and they must plan for these times. During economic downturns, construction activity is significantly reduced, and jobs for construction craft workers, including glaziers, become scarce. Also, construction jobs are almost always of limited length, and workers may be unemployed between projects. On the other hand, when the level of construction activity is high in a region, there may be more jobs available than there are skilled workers to fill them. In general, jobs will be most abundant in and near cities, where most glazing contractors and glass shops are located.

In addition to newly created jobs, many openings will develop every year as experienced workers change to other occupations or leave the labor force altogether.

Earnings

Earnings of glaziers are very different in different parts of the country. A recent study suggests that annual earnings can average from about $20,000 to about $40,000, depending on geographical location. In another sampling of wages, hourly wages of union workers averaged $24.00, including fringe benefits, and ranged from $16.00 (in Birmingham, Alabama) to $34.00 (in New York City). However, bad weather, periods of unemployment, and other factors can mean that the number of hours glaziers work, and thus their real earnings, are considerably lower than the high hourly figures suggest.

Glaziers who work under union contracts usually make more money than workers who are not union members. Wages for apprentices usually start at about 50 percent of the skilled glazier's rate and increase periodically throughout the training period.

Conditions of Work

Most glaziers work in construction, renovation, and repair of buildings and are employed by construction companies, glass suppliers, or glazing contractors. Working on buildings may require them to be outdoors, sometimes in unpleasant weather. Bad weather can also cause the shutdown of job activities, limiting the hours glaziers work and thus also limiting their pay. Glaziers typically work forty-hour weeks and receive compensation for overtime.

Glaziers in construction often have to work at great heights, on scaffolding, or in buildings that are not yet completed. On the job, they must frequently bend, kneel, lift objects, and move about. The hazards they must be careful to guard against include cuts from broken glass, falls from heights, and muscle strains caused by using improper techniques to lift heavy pieces of glass.

Glaziers who are employed by construction companies, glass suppliers, or glazing contractors may have to drive trucks that carry glass and tools to and from job sites.

Sources of Additional Information

■ **Glazing Contractors Association**
840 Weston Street
Coquitlam, BC V3J 529 Canada
Tel: 604-931-2725

■ **International Brotherhood of Painters and Allied Trades**
United Nations Building
1750 New York Avenue, NW
Washington, DC 20006
Tel: 202-637-0700

Ironworkers

School Subjects
Mathematics
Shop (Trade/Vo-tech education)

Personal Interests
Building things
Fixing things

Work Environment
Primarily outdoors
Primarily multiple locations

Minimum Education Level
High school diploma
Apprenticeship

Salary Range
$20,000 to $80,000

Certification or Licensing
None

Outlook
As fast as the average

Definition

Ironworkers fabricate, assemble, and install structural and reinforcing metal products used in the construction of buildings and bridges. They also install steel walls, iron stairways, and other metal components of buildings; assemble large metal tanks for chemicals, water, and oil; and do similar structural work with other metals.

History

Many important developments in the methods for producing iron and steel took place during the Industrial Revolution. In the eighteenth century, new processes for smelting iron ore and shaping iron and steel in mills improved the quality of metal products and encouraged the development of new uses for metals. The first all-iron bridge was built in England in 1779. A hundred years later, steel had almost completely replaced iron as the principal structural material for bridges. Steel, which is much stronger and lighter than iron, was first used as a structural element in buildings in the early nineteenth century. After that, steel beams and other steel members made possible an increasingly ambitious variety of structures. By the end of the century, the use of structural steel was part of a whole new approach to building construction.

One new architectural form that evolved during this period was the skyscraper, with its steel skeleton. Tall buildings were a natural application for the new technology, because the first safe passenger elevators were developed in this era, and in many cities growing commerce was crowding small central business districts. In 1883, steel girders were used for the first time in a tall building, a nearly all-metal, ten-story structure in Chicago. The 984-foot-tall Eiffel Tower, completed in 1889, was built of steel girders. Taller and taller buildings were erected in a race for the highest structure that did not slow until the Great Depression and World War II.

Today, many buildings, especially low-rise industrial and commercial buildings, are made with prefabricated metal parts assembled at the site by skilled workers. Steel components are made by companies that specialize in producing these products in standard configurations that can be adapted for individual buildings. Another building material today is steel-reinforced concrete, which is often fabricated at the site. The reinforcing metal may be steel bars or wire fabric. The technology of steel-reinforced concrete developed more slowly than all-steel construction in the late nineteenth and early twentieth centuries. However, it is now probably the most frequently used building material in many countries around the world.

Steel and other metals, including iron, aluminum, and bronze, are also used in erecting bridges, highways, power transmission towers, piers, and many other structures. Ironworkers are skilled in fabricating, assembling, and installing such structures. They also repair and maintain older structures including steel mills, automobile plants, highways, and bridges.

Nature of the Work

Structural ironworkers work as members of crews, usually a team of five people. They often work high above the ground as they raise, place, and join together different combinations of steel components, such as girders and columns, into completed structures or frameworks. At a construction site, they begin by setting up cranes and derricks that will be used to move structural steel, buckets of concrete, reinforcing steel bars, lumber, and other materials. This hoisting equipment is usually delivered to the site in sections that must be joined together.

Next the workers start laying out the steel building components. They follow blueprints and instructions from supervisors. Structural steel, reinforcing bars, and other parts are usually delivered to the site already cut to the correct size, with holes drilled for bolts, and numbered so they can be easily identified. The workers at the site usually need only to bolt and weld the pieces together. They unload and identify the steel for assembly, stacking the pieces so they will be available when needed.

When it is time to lift a piece of steel into position, the workers fasten it to cables on the crane or derrick. One worker (called the *pusher* or *foreman*) hand signals to the *crane operator;* another (the *hook-on man*) applies the choker around the iron so that it is secure and has good balance; and another (the *tag line man*) hooks on to the iron being erected, using a line with a small iron hook to guide the iron to the connectors. The *connectors*, up in the air where the steel is being erected, guide the steel into the approximate position, pushing, pulling, and prying if necessary. Then they position the steel more exactly by aligning the holes in it with the framework that is already in place. They secure it temporarily, holding it with drift pins or a special wrench. Before the steel is fastened in place, they verify its horizontal and vertical alignment, using plumb bobs, laser equipment, transits, and levels. Finally they bolt or weld the steel member permanently in place.

Ornamental ironworkers assemble and install metal stairways, floor gratings, ladders, railings, catwalks, window frames, fences, lampposts, and other metal structures that may be decorative as well as functional. Usually the metal is prefabricated and hoisted into place after the building framework is completed. The workers must align them with the structure, then bolt, braze, or weld them securely in place.

Reinforcing ironworkers, or *rodmen,* set reinforcing metal bars or wire fabric into concrete forms before the concrete is poured, giving the cured concrete greater strength. Based on sketches, blueprints, or oral instructions from supervisors, the workers determine the number, size, shape, and intended location of the metal reinforcements. Although the metal is usually delivered to the site already shaped, the workers may have to shape it further. They may fasten bars together by using pliers to wrap wire around them. Sometimes they must cut the metal, using metal shears or acetylene torches. They may bend bars, by hand or using rod-bending machines, and they may weld bars together. Once the reinforcing metal is prepared, they set it in place in the concrete forms. For concrete floors, they must put supports under the metal to hold it off the deck. A concrete crew puts the wet concrete in place. As the concrete goes in, ironworkers may position wire fabric in place using hooked rods.

Ironworker riggers usually work on special rigging jobs where they use biber line, wire rope, chains and hooks, slings and guylines, hoisting equipment, anchorages, scaffolding, and skids and rollers to lift and move loads. These ironworkers must be able to tie special knots and hitches and make splices.

Other workers in this field include *tank setters,* who erect metal tanks used to store crude oil at oil fields. *Metal building assemblers* assemble prefabricated buildings. Following blueprints and specifications, they bolt the steel frames together, attach sheet-metal panels to the framework, cut openings, and install doors, windows, and ventilators. Some ironworkers work in fabricating shops away from the site where metal products will eventually be used. They lay out raw steel from mills and cut, bend, drill, and weld pieces together in accordance with specifications for particular jobs.

Requirements

Ironworkers may learn their skills by completing an apprenticeship, or they may learn informally on the job. Apprenticeships are the preferred method, because apprentices usually receive more complete training in a shorter period of time. For either kind of training, workers need to be at least eighteen years old. A high school diploma is desirable and may be required. A good background for this kind of work would include high school courses in shop, mechanical drawing, blueprint reading, and applied mathematics.

Apprenticeships combine a planned on-the-job training program with classroom instruction in related subjects. They last three years and include at least 144 hours of classroom instruction each year. On the job, apprentices work under the supervision of skilled workers. They learn all the different aspects of the trade, including unloading and arranging materials at job sites, rigging steel for lifting with hoisting equipment, techniques for connecting steel to the building framework, use of measuring equipment to verify position, and welding. In the classroom, they learn such subjects as blueprint reading, mathematics for layout work, the basics of erecting and assembling structures, job safety practices, and the use and care of tools. Apprenticeships are usually run by joint committees representing local branches of contractors' associations and locals of the union to which these workers often belong, the International Association of Bridge, Structural and Ornamental Ironworkers.

Workers who learn informally on the job usually start as helpers to experienced workers. They begin with simple tasks, like carrying materials, and work up to the more difficult tasks, like fitting steel sections together. Unlike apprentices, they do not have the benefit of classroom instruction, but some employers have thorough training programs.

Ironworkers need to be agile, able to climb, stoop, crouch, reach, and kneel. They must be in good physical condition, with good eyesight, including depth perception, good coordination and balance, and, perhaps most importantly for ironworkers on skyscrapers, they should not be afraid of heights! In many jobs, they need strength enough to lift very heavy weights and stamina to keep active for much of the workday.

Opportunities for Experience & Exploration

High school students can begin to gauge their interest in this field by taking courses in mathematics, mechanical drawing, blueprint reading, and shop. A course that introduces welding would be especially useful, because that skill is often used by these workers. It is not easy to get a part-time or temporary job in this field. However, perhaps with the help of a teacher or guidance counselor, it may be possible to visit a construction site where ironworkers are employed.

Methods of Entering

Those who would like to enter this field as apprentices should contact the local offices of the International Association of Bridge, Structural and Ornamental Ironworkers for details on applying for apprenticeship positions. Information about apprenticeships, as well as about job openings for nonapprentice helpers in this field, may be obtained through the local offices of the state employment service. Job seekers can also apply directly to local structural steel erection and reinforcing steel contractors and other contractors that may be hiring for helper positions.

Advancement

Skilled and experienced ironworkers may be considered for positions as supervisors, directing the activities of a crew of other ironworkers. With additional education, a good knowledge of other construction trades, and judgment and leadership qualities, workers may advance to become job superintendents. Experienced workers also can establish their own businesses.

94

Employment Outlook

There are currently about 140,000 workers employed in this field. Over the next ten to fifteen years, this number should increase at about the same rate as the average for all other occupations. This increase will be related to a growing demand for industrial and commercial buildings, as well as to the need to rehabilitate and maintain older structures such as highways, bridges, and manufacturing and power plants. In addition, many job openings will become available each year when experienced workers transfer to other jobs or leave the workforce.

Like workers in other construction trades, ironworkers can expect job opportunities to vary with economic conditions. When the overall economy is in a downturn, construction activity usually falls noticeably, and these workers may face longer periods between construction projects. They may have to relocate to other areas to find steadier employment. Because construction usually picks up during the warm months, there are usually more jobs available during the spring and summer.

Earnings

Annual earnings for ironworkers range from $35,000 to $80,000, assuming they can work full time. Workers may lose hours during bad weather, and their earnings are reduced if they must be out of work between jobs. Overtime can boost earnings somewhat.

Apprentices start at 40 to 60 percent of the skilled worker's rate (about $20,000) and receive periodic increases during their training.

Conditions of Work

Most ironworkers are employed by large construction companies located in large cities. Most of the work is done outdoors, in varying weather conditions. Although some of the job is done at great heights, workers do not go high above the ground during icy, wet, or very windy weather.

Because of the danger of falling, these workers always use safety nets, belts, scaffolding, or other safety equipment. They also must be constantly careful to avoid being hit by falling objects.

Sources of Additional Information

■ **Associated General Contractors of America**
1957 E Street, NW
Washington, DC 20006
Tel: 202-393-2040
Email: 73264.15@compuserv.com
WWW: http://agc.org

■ **International Association of Bridge, Structural and Ornamental Ironworkers**
1750 New York Avenue, NW
Washington, DC 20006
Tel: 202-383-4800

■ **National Association of Reinforcing Steel Contractors**
10382 Main Street, Suite 300
Fairfax, VA 22030
Tel: 703-591-1870

■ **National Erectors Association**
1501 Lee Highway, #202
Arlington, VA 22209
Tel: 703-524-3336

Lathers

School Subjects
Mathematics
Shop (Trade/Vo-tech education)

Personal Interests
Building things
Fixing things

Work Environment
Indoors and outdoors
Primarily multiple locations

Minimum Education Level
High school diploma
Apprenticeship

Salary Range
$12,000 to $45,000

Certification or Licensing
None

Outlook
Little change or more slowly than the average

DOT: 840   **GOE:** 05.10.01   **NOC:** 7284

Definition

Lathers work specifically with lath, which is any material fastened to a building's structural bases (such as walls, ceilings, and roofs) to provide a foundation for the application of such things as plaster, tile, roofing material, fireproofing, and acoustical material. (Lathers should not be confused with machinists, who work on power-driven equipment called lathes.)

History

The lather's craft as we know it today did not become established until the late nineteenth century. Using support bases on walls and roofs of buildings as a foundation for other materials and to retain warmth, however, is a method that comes from old ideas. In the Middle East and in Europe there is evidence that ancient buildings were being made with a method called wattle and daub, a precursor to lathing.

The wattle and daub method, one of the oldest known processes used for weatherproofing structures, was used in England at least as far back as the Iron Age. In this construction process, wooden stakes, called wattles, were set vertically into the ground, rods and twigs were horizontally woven through the wattles, and this base was then covered, or daubed, with clay or mud. During the Middle Ages, houses in Europe were often constructed in this way.

By the end of medieval times, lathing was already being practiced as an alternative to wattle and daub. Laths were made of thin strips of wood (most commonly oak) nailed across a dwelling's rafters to support the roofing material (which was made of thatch, tiles, or lead); such laths were also used on walls as a support for plaster. The production of laths was an industry in itself, as these supports began to be implemented in all types of structures and used in great quantities. For example, it is recorded that eighty-seven thousand laths were used in reconstruction of the London Bridge in the fourteenth century; fifty-seven thousand were made from the inner heart of the oak (heartlath), and thirty thousand were made from the outer, sappy wood (saplath).

As the centuries passed, different materials replaced wood as the material of choice for laths. By the early part of the twentieth century, construction of large commercial buildings and apartment houses provided lathers with many opportunities to use their craft. Since that time, lathing and plastering materials and methods have rapidly developed. The most common lath materials besides wood have been metal and gypsum (plasterboard).

Nature of the Work

Wherever there is building construction, lathers are found installing metal lath (woven or welded wire or expanded metal) or large pieces of gypsum lath as supportive backings for interior and exterior walls, ceilings, and roofs. Material called blue board is also used as a lath for the application of veneer plaster, a relatively new product.

Metal laths are made in mesh form and are used often for kitchens and bathrooms, where tile walls are frequently built; the mesh is attached to a structural base, and plaster is affixed to the mesh so that tiles can be set in securely. Gypsum is made of several layers of fiberboard, paper, or felt bonded to a hard plaster core; it is used as a backing or substitute for plaster. Board that is made with reflective sheets of foil is also used in lathing as insulation and as a barrier against moisture.

The metal lath process includes three steps. First, the lather builds a light framework called furring that is fastened securely to the structural framework of the building. Second, the lath is attached to this furring with screws, nails, wires, clips, or staples. Third, the lather cuts openings in the lath for heating and ventilating pipes and ducts for electrical outlets. The gypsum lath process is similar to the process using metal except that this board comes in large panels and must be cut by the lather to fit small and odd-shaped areas.

In addition to installing lath as support backings for walls, lathers also install corner beads (metal reinforcements used as corner protections and as guides for plasterers) and the wire mesh around steel beams to which plaster is applied for fireproofing. Sometimes their work also includes installing wooden backings for acoustical ceilings and wall tiles.

Lathers are often known by the type of lath specialized in—*metal lathers* and *wood lathers,* for example. They use many tools, including measuring rules and tapes, hammers, chisels, hacksaws, shears, wire cutters, bolt cutters, pliers, hatchets, stapling machines, wood and metal drills, and drywall tools (for blue board).

Before becoming skilled professionals, workers are involved in formal, standardized training programs during which they are known as lather apprentices. As in other industries, the apprentice is responsible for learning the specified skills involved in his or her craft. Apprentice lathers must attend classes to learn all aspects of the trade, including characteristics of the materials and tools used; mathematics as applied to calculating and estimating measurements; and blueprint reading. After attending a certain amount of classroom instruction, apprentices are assigned to work for employers in the capacity of helpers to professional lathers and are provided with a progressive wage scale.

Requirements

Most employers prefer to hire workers with a high school diploma or the equivalent (i.e., general equivalency diploma or GED). Lathers are responsible for taking many measurements and calculating equations to fit laths properly. Thus, the high school student's preparation should include courses in geometry and applied mathematics as well as shop classes. Lathers must have a high degree of manual dexterity so that they can use their tools effectively. They should be able to work well on their own as well as with others. Patience, accuracy, and attention to detail are also essential.

To qualify as a skilled professional lather, a person usually completes an apprenticeship program. The apprenticeship program consists of seven thousand hours of carefully planned activity combining on-the-job work experience with formal classroom instruction, which equals about three and a half years of study. After each six-month period, apprentices must pass specific examinations. It is also possible to become a lather by starting as a helper and learning the trade entirely on the job. Workers who pursue this route normally become professional lathers after four or five years.

Opportunities for Experience & Exploration

During high school, students have several avenues open to them for exploring the occupation of lather. Courses in metal shop, wood shop, and mechanical drawing will test their ability and aptitude for this kind of work, whereas courses in geometry and mathematics will gauge their skill in making calculations. Furthermore, hobbies such as carpentry, which requires working with a variety of tools, will provide valuable practical experience with this work.

To observe the lather at work, field trips to construction sites can be arranged by the school counselor, or students may make such arrangements on their own. An excellent opportunity for exploring this occupation would be a part-time summer job as a helper or assistant to a skilled lather.

Methods of Entering

Apprenticeship programs are essentially the most direct route to lathing occupations. Such programs provide potential employees with a formal method of acquiring the standard skills necessary in the field.

Those who wish to become apprentices usually contact employers (such as lathing and plastering contractors), the state apprenticeship agency, or the appropriate local union headquarters (e.g., the United Brotherhood of Carpenters and Joiners of America). However, applicants must have the approval of the joint apprenticeship committee before they can enter the occupation by this method.

If the desired apprenticeship program is filled, applicants might wish to enter the field directly as on-the-job trainees. In this case, they usually contact the employer and begin work as helpers.

Advancement

After increasing their skill and efficiency for several years, professional lathers have various promotional opportunities open to them. They may specialize in working with a specific lath and thus become a metal lather, *gypsum lather,* or wood lather. If they have certain personal characteristics—such as good judgment and planning skills and the ability to deal effectively with people—lathers can be promoted to such positions as supervisor, job superintendent, or job estimator. Also, lathers who have enough financial resources and business knowledge can eventually go into business for themselves.

Employment Outlook

About twenty-eight thousand lathers are employed in the United States, the majority of whom work for lathing and plastering contractors on new residential, commercial, or industrial construction. Most jobs are located in metropolitan and other urban areas. (Where work assignments are scarce, such as in rural areas, the lathing function is usually performed by carpenters or painters.)

Population increases and business growth tend to stimulate the construction and renovation of buildings, and such trends often have a positive impact on the demand for lathers. The U.S. Department of Labor anticipates that, through the year 2005, job opportunities for lathers will increase at a rate on par with that for all occupations. But most jobs will result from the need to replace workers who retire, transfer, or leave the occupation for other reasons.

In the recent past, the increased use of drywall (a good substitute for, and less expensive than, lath and plaster) as a wall covering material meant that the demand for drywall installers went up, while the demand for lathers declined. Currently, however, the development of new lathing products has made veneer plaster more desirable than drywall, and as a result lathers have begun to use this material instead of the usual metal or gypsum. (It is said by some that drywallers may come and go, but lathers stay in the trade.)

Earnings

Some contractors pay lathers according to how many lath panels they install per day; others pay an hourly rate. The earnings of experienced lathers vary according to different geographic regions, but the average hourly wage rates compare favorably with others in the skilled building trades.

During the 1990s, average weekly earnings for lathers are about $500, which is about $24,000 annually. Experienced lathers can make up to $45,000. Apprentices receive about 50 percent of the rate paid to experienced lathers, with periodic increases.

Union contracts often include health and life insurance, pension plans, and other benefits, financed either entirely by the employers or jointly by the workers and the employers.

Conditions of Work

Most lathers work a standard forty-hour week, and they earn extra pay for overtime. The work is performed both indoors and outdoors in all kinds of weather on construction sites, which are generally not heated. As in many of the building trades, lathers are subject to seasonal layoffs.

Much of a lather's workday is spent on his or her feet, often on ladders and scaffolds. Possible hazards of the trade include cuts, falls, strains from lifting heavy objects, and injuries from power tools.

Sources of Additional Information

■ **Association of the Wall and Ceiling Industries International**
307 East Annandale Road
Falls Church, VA 22042
Tel: 703-534-8300

■ **International Institute for Lath and Plaster**
25322 Narbonne Avenue
Washington, DC 20002
Tel: 202-393-6569

■ **United Brotherhood of Carpenters and Joiners of America**
101 Constitution Avenue, NW
Washington, DC 20001
Tel: 202-546-6206

Marble Setters, Tile Setters, and Terrazzo Workers

School Subjects
Art
Shop (Trade/Vo-tech education)

Personal Interests
Building things
Drawing/painting

Work Environment
Indoors and outdoors
Primarily multiple locations

Minimum Education Level
High school diploma
Apprenticeship

Salary Range
$16,000 to $50,000

Certification or Licensing
None

Outlook
About as fast as the average

DOT: 861   **NOC:** 7219

Definition

Marble setters, tile setters, and *terrazzo workers* cover interior or exterior walls, floors, or other surfaces with marble, tile, or terrazzo. Workers in each of these distinct trades work primarily with the material indicated by their title.

History

The temples of Greece and the ruins of Rome are testimony to the fact that marble and granite have been used as building materials for thousands of years. It has been difficult through the years to find a longer-lasting material than marble, which, at the same time, is soft enough to be cut to size. For this reason sculptors have used marble for busts and statues. Marble, a limestone, is quarried or mined in many countries of the world.

Terrazzo—small pieces of broken stone set in mortar and polished in place—was developed as a building material by the Venetians in the 1500s. Today this very decorative technique is used mainly for flooring.

Products such as steel and concrete have generally replaced marble as a building material, although marble continues to be used on the interiors and to some extent on the exteriors of commercial, government, and institutional buildings. In the minds of many people, marble buildings exude a timeless quality of strength and security. There are still enough architects in America who agree that the future of marble as an exterior construction material is ensured, however reduced in use it may be.

Nature of the Work

Half builders and half artists, marble setters, tile setters, and terrazzo workers work on newly constructed or remodeled buildings. Tile and terrazzo are used mainly on interior building surfaces, while marble (in large pieces) is used primarily as exterior facing.

In marble work, the material to be used is generally delivered to the site ready to be applied, so little cutting and polishing are required. Machine hoists aid in lifting large marble blocks. Helpers do most of the human lifting and carrying, as well as the mixing of cement and mortar, which leaves the applicators free to concentrate on their work. It only takes one look at a wall that was improperly laid (where the joint lines do not run true) to realize the importance of accuracy for these workers. Where color is used, the appearance of the whole job can be ruined by an improper blending of hues.

When setting marble, the workers first lay out the job. Then they apply a special plaster mixture to the backing material and set the marble pieces in place. These pieces may have to be braced until they are firmly in place. Special grout is packed into the joints between the marble pieces, and the joints are slightly indented. This indenting is known as "pointing up."

Tile setters attach tile (thin slabs of clay or stone) to floors or walls with mortar or specially prepared tile cement. Some smaller-sized tile comes in sheets made by fastening a number of tiles to a special paper backing so that they do not have to be set individually. Glassy, nonporous tile is used primarily for floors, and duller, more porous tile for walls.

Terrazzo workers lay a base (first course) of fine, dry concrete and level it with a straightedge. They then place metal strips wherever a joint will be placed or where design or color delineations are to be made. This metal stripping is embedded in the first course of concrete. Then the terrazzo workers pour the top course of concrete—a mortar containing marble or granite chips—and roll and level it. Different colored stone chips are used to color whatever pattern has been planned for the finished floor. In a few days, after the concrete has hardened, the floor is ground smooth and polished with large polishing machines.

Unlike many construction jobs, these occupations are relatively free from routine. Each job is slightly different, and workers rely on their training and ingenuity to a great extent. Marble setters, tile setters, and terrazzo workers generally do not have immediate supervisors on the job. They manage their own time, schedule their work, and have the responsibility of doing whatever is necessary to provide the best possible job. Because these workers have an opportunity to plan the job, see that the material is delivered on time, and follow the work through the cleanup phase, they often feel a greater sense of satisfaction from the completed job than construction workers who are responsible for only one part of the total job.

Requirements

Persons wishing to apply for jobs in these three trades should be at least seventeen years of age to qualify for labor-management apprenticeship programs. They should also have a high school education or a GED, with some courses that involve using hand tools, reading blueprints, and taking precise measurements. Art courses will increase the worker's knowledge and perception of colors, and many vocational courses will improve manual dexterity. In addition, good physical condition is a necessity.

Apprenticeship programs in each of these trades usually consist of about six thousand hours or three years of on-the-job training and related classroom instruction. During this time apprentices learn how to use the tools of their particular trade plus blueprint reading, layout work, basic mathematics, and shop practice. Most workers in these trades belong to unions.

Opportunities for Experience & Exploration

Young people still in school may be able to obtain summer work as laborers at construction sites or for general contractors. The work may include mixing mortar, carrying, lifting, and cleanup work. By working with master craft workers and asking questions, a person begins to learn the trade. This is also a good way to make personal connections that will be helpful in finding work.

Methods of Entering

Although a formal three-year apprenticeship has been established in each of these trades, a large percentage of workers learn the work informally by working a certain number of years as a helper, learning the work firsthand from experienced craftspeople.

People interested in this work should first contact prospective employers. In addition, the local office of the state employment service may be a source of additional information about the Manpower and Development Training Act, apprenticeship training, and other programs.

After being accepted for a job, new employees are referred for clearance to the union and, after a period of time working, are given positions as helpers. When an opening occurs for a skilled worker, the best qualified person with the most seniority is recommended for the position.

Advancement

Skilled tile, terrazzo, or marble setters may become supervisors with the responsibility of managing work crews for large contractors. They can also become self-employed and do contracting on their own. Self-employed contractors must know not only the skills of the trade but also the principles of business. These skills include sales, bidding, bookkeeping, the ways to make and keep a business on a firm financial footing, and supervising workers.

Employment Outlook

Employment for marble setters, tile setters, and terrazzo workers will increase about as fast as the average rate over the next decade. Of course, marble, tile, or terrazzo workers can expand their employment opportunities by moving to more populated urban and suburban areas where more buildings are being constructed and remodeled. Workers may find that work is steadier in climates that allow year-round construction. Terrazzo is particularly popular in Florida and California.

Earnings

Median annual wages for tile setters are about $46,800, marble setters about $33,000, and terrazzo workers about $32,000. Wages vary with geographic location, with the highest rates paid in urban areas.

Apprentices start at about 50 percent of the skilled worker's salary and increase periodically up to 95 percent during the final stage of the training. Many opportunities exist for overtime work, which usually pays workers time-and-a-half, or one-and-a-half times the regular wage. Most workers are union members and are eligible for the retirement and hospital insurance benefits of the union.

Conditions of Work

Tile setters work mostly inside, while marble and terrazzo workers work both indoors and outdoors. Work is often demanding, requiring some strength and physical fitness.

Sources of Additional Information

■ **International Union of Bricklayers and Allied Craftsmen**
815 15th Street, NW
Washington, DC 20005
Tel: 202-783-3788

■ **National Terrazzo and Mosaic Association**
3166 Des Plaines Avenue, Suite 121
Des Plaines, IL 60018
Tel: 847-635-7744

■ **Operative Plasterers and Cement Masons International Association of the United States and Canada**
1125 17th Street, NW
Washington, DC 20036
Tel: 202-383-6569

■ **United Brotherhood of Carpenters and Joiners of America**
101 Constitution Avenue, NW
Washington, DC 20001
Tel: 202-546-6206

Operating Engineers

School Subjects
Mathematics
Shop (Trade/Vo-tech education)

Personal Interests
Building things
Fixing things

Work Environment
Primarily outdoors
Primarily multiple locations

Minimum Education Level
High school diploma
Apprenticeship

Salary Range
$13,000 to $39,000

Certification or Licensing
None

Outlook
About as fast as the average

DOT: 859   **GOE:** 05.11.01   **NOC:** 7421

Definition

Operating engineers operate various types of power-driven construction machines such as shovels, cranes, tractors, bulldozers, pile drivers, concrete mixers, and pumps.

History

Although it is not understood precisely how it was accomplished, the ancient Egyptians used some type of hoisting system to move the giant stone blocks of the pyramids into place. The Romans constructed roads, viaducts, and bridges of high quality, many of which are still in use today. The Great Wall of China, begun in the third century BC, remains an amazing architectural feat and is one of the few man-made structures visible from space.

These ancient marvels of engineering are even more amazing when one considers that they were all built using only human muscle and simple machines such as levers and pulleys. It was not until the Industrial Revolution and the invention of the steam engine that complex machines were extensively used in construction. After the harnessing of steam power, Western Europe and America made rapid progress in constructing buildings, roads, and water and sewerage systems.

Construction has always played an important role in history. Today many people measure progress by the increase in new construction in a town or city. All sizes and shapes of construction machinery have been introduced in recent years, and *operating engineers* have worked hard to stay current in their training and abilities.

Nature of the Work

Operating engineers work for contractors who build highways, dams, airports, skyscrapers, buildings, and other large-scale projects. Others work for utility companies, manufacturers, factories, mines, steel mills, and other firms that do their own construction work. Many work for state and local public works and highway departments.

Whatever the company, operating engineers run power shovels, cranes, derricks, hoists, pile drivers, concrete mixers, paving machines, trench excavators, bulldozers, tractors, and pumps. They use these machines to move construction materials, earth, logs, coal, grain, and other material. Generally, operating engineers move the materials over short distances—around a construction site, factory, or warehouse, or on and off trucks and ships. They also do minor repairs on the equipment, as well as keep them fueled and lubricated. They are often identified by the machines they operate.

Bulldozer operators operate the familiar bulldozer, a tractor-like vehicle with a large blade across the front for moving rocks, trees, earth, and other obstacles from construction sites. They also operate trench excavators, road graders, and similar equipment.

Crane and tower operators lift and move materials, machinery, or other heavy objects with mechanical booms and tower and cable equipment. Although some cranes are used on construction sites, most are used in manufacturing and other industries.

Excavation and loading machine operators handle machinery equipped with scoops, shovels, or buckets to excavate earth at construction sites and to load and move loose materials, mainly in the construction and mining industries.

Hoist and winch operators lift and pull heavy loads using power-operated equipment. Most work in loading operations in construction, manufacturing, logging, transportation and public utilities, and mining.

Operating engineers use various pedals, levers, and switches to run their machinery. For example, *crane operators* may rotate a crane on its chassis, lift and lower its boom, or lift and lower the load. They also use various attachments to the boom such as buckets, pile drivers, or heavy wrecking balls. When a tall building is being constructed, the crane and its operator may be positioned several hundred feet off the ground.

Operating engineers must have very precise knowledge about the capabilities and limitations of the machines they operate. To avoid tipping over their cranes or damaging their loads, crane operators must be able to judge distance and height and estimate their load size. They must be able to raise and lower the loads with great accuracy. Sometimes the operator cannot see the point where the load is to be picked up or delivered. At these times, they follow the directions of other workers using hand or flag signals or radio transmissions.

The range of skills of the operating engineer is broader than in most building trades, because the machines themselves differ in the ways they operate and the jobs they do. Some operators know how to work several types of machines, while others specialize with one machine.

Requirements

A high school education or the equivalent technical training is valuable for the operating engineer and is a requirement for apprenticeship training. It is important that the operator has excellent mechanical aptitude and skillful coordination of eye, hand, and foot movements. In addition, because reckless use of the machinery may be dangerous to other workers, it is necessary to have a good sense of responsibility and seriousness on the job.

There are two ways to become an operating engineer: through the union apprentice program or through on-the-job training. The apprenticeship, which lasts three years, has at least two advantages: the instruction is more complete, which results in greater employment opportunities; and both labor and management know that the apprentice is training to be an operating engineer.

Besides learning on the job, the apprentice also receives some classroom instruction in grade-plans reading, elements of electricity, physics, welding, and lubrication services. It must be remembered that most apprenticeship programs are difficult to enter because the number of apprentices is limited to the number of skilled workers already in the field.

Operating engineers should be healthy and strong. They need the temperament to withstand dirt and noise as well as changing weather conditions. To apply to an apprenticeship program, a candidate generally must be between the ages of eighteen and thirty. Many operating engineers belong to the International Union of Operating Engineers.

Opportunities for Experience & Exploration

Young people can sometimes gain practical experience by operating machines or by observing them in action through summer jobs as a laborer or machine operator's helper in construction work. Such jobs may be available on local, state, and federal highway and building construction programs.

Methods of Entering

Once apprentices complete their training and become journeyworkers, their names are put on a list; as positions open up, they are filled in order from the list of available workers. For those people who are not interested in an apprenticeship program, they may apply directly to manufacturers, utilities, or contractors who employ operating engineers in the hopes of getting a job as a machine operator's helper.

Advancement

Some operating engineers—generally those with above-average ability and interest, as well as good working habits—advance to job supervisor and occasionally construction supervisor. Some are able to qualify for higher pay by training themselves to operate more complicated machines.

Employment Outlook

Approximately three hundred thousand operating engineers are employed today. Increased spending planned for the nation's infrastructure means the employment outlook is good for this category. Employment of all operating engineers is projected to grow about as fast as the average. Employment of hoist and winch operators and of *industrial truck and tractor operators* is to expected grow more slowly than average, however, because of increased efficiency brought about by automation (factories and plants are increasingly relying on computer-controlled material handling systems, many of which do not require a human operator).

About 75 percent of the operating engineers work in construction and local government—industries that are associated with the construction and repair of highways, bridges, dams, harbors, airports, subways, water and sewage systems, and power plants and transmission lines. Construction of schools, office and other commercial buildings, and residential property will also stimulate demand for these workers. However, the construction industry is very sensitive to changes in the overall economy, so the number of openings may fluctuate from year to year.

Earnings

The median annual salary for all operating engineers is about $22,000. Rates vary according to the area of the country and also according to the machine being operated. Crane and tower operators earn a median annual salary of $28,800; excavation and loading machine operators, $24,000; bulldozer operators, $23,000; and other material moving equipment operators, $21,000. The wage scale is further complicated by the experience of the operator and the purpose for which the machine is being used.

Conditions of Work

Operating engineers consider dirt and noise a part of their jobs. Some of the machines on which they work constantly shake and jolt them. This constant movement, along with the strenuous, outdoor nature of the work, makes this a physically tiring job. Since the work is done almost entirely outdoors in almost any kind of weather, operating engineers must be willing to work under conditions that are often unpleasant.

Sources of Additional Information

■ **Associated General Contractors of America**
1957 E Street, NW
Washington, DC 20006
Tel: 202-393-2040
Email: 73264.15@compuserv
WWW: http://agc.org

■ **International Union of Operating Engineers**
1125 17th Street, NW
Washington, DC 20036
Tel: 202-429-9100

Painters and Paperhangers

School Subjects
Mathematics
Shop (Trade/Vo-tech education)

Personal Interests
Building things
Drawing/painting

Work Environment
Indoors and outdoors
Primarily multiple locations

Minimum Education Level
High school diploma
Apprenticeship

Salary Range
$12,000 to $38,000

Certification or Licensing
None

Outlook
Faster than the average

DOT: 840   **GOE:** 05.10.07

Definition

For both practical purposes and aesthetic appeal, building surfaces are often painted and decorated with various types of coverings. Although painting and paperhanging are two separate skills, many building trades craft workers do both types of work. *Painters* apply paints, varnishes, enamels, and other types of finishes to decorate and protect interior and exterior surfaces of buildings and other structures. *Paperhangers* cover interior walls and ceilings with decorative paper, fabric, vinyls, and other types of materials.

History

In examining the background of the painter's trade, consider the many old houses from the eighteenth century, for example, that still stand today. Nearly all such houses have a buildup of layers of paint, on both the exterior siding and the interior walls and ceilings. If you were to scrape the walls of such surfaces, you might find at least twenty-five coats of paint! In some rooms, the layers are so thick that you can barely see the carved designs in the moldings (the decorative wood strips around ceilings and floors). Whenever a building's owner wanted a change, or when the paint began to look weathered, a new coat of paint would be applied.

The history of the skilled house painter's occupation in this country begins in the eighteenth century, when American colonists made their own paints for use on their homes. There were few people in the business of manufacturing paint in the colonies, and it was unusual to order materials from other countries because the shipping and transport industries were not as sophisticated as they are today.

Builders and owners instead depended on local products for making paint. Milk, for example, was often used as a base. Soil from land that had traces of iron was burned to make paint with a red pigment, or colored tint. Material called lampblack, which is black soot, was also used to make pigmented paint. In 1867, manufacturers made available the first prepared paints.

After this, machines were invented to enable manufacturers to produce paint in large amounts. Paperhanging as an occupation probably began around the sixteenth century. Although the Chinese invented decorative paper, it was the Europeans who first used it to cover walls. Wealthy homeowners often decorated the walls of their rooms with tapestries and velvet hangings (which was often done for warmth as well as decoration); those who could not afford such luxuries would imitate the rich by hanging inexpensive, yet decorative, wallpaper in their homes.

Paperhangers and painters were in great demand as building construction developed on a large scale in the early part of the twentieth century. Since the middle of the century, there have been great advancements in the materials and techniques used by these skilled trades workers.

Nature of the Work

Workers in the painting and paperhanging trades often perform both functions; painters will often take on jobs that involve hanging wallpaper, and paperhangers will sometimes work in situations where they are responsible for painting walls and ceilings. However, although there is some overlap in the work done by painters and paperhangers, each trade has its own characteristic skills.

Painters must be able to apply paint thoroughly, uniformly, and rapidly to any type of surface. To do this, they must be skilled in handling brushes and other painting tools and have a working knowledge of the various characteristics of paints and finishes—their durability, suitability, and ease of handling and application.

Preparation of the area to be painted is an important duty of painters, especially when repainting old surfaces. They first smooth the surface, removing old, loose paint with a scraper, paint remover (usually a liquid solution), a wire brush, or paint removing gun (similar in appearance to a blowdryer for hair), or a combination of several of these items. If necessary, they must also remove grease and fill nail holes, cracks, and joints with putty, plaster, or other types of filler. Often, a prime coat or a sealer is applied to further smooth the surface and make the finished coat level and well blended in color.

Once the surface is prepared, painters select premixed paints or prepare paint themselves by mixing required portions of pigment, oil, and thinning and drying substances. (For purposes of preparing paint, workers must have a thorough knowledge of the composition of the various materials they use and of which materials mix well together.) They then paint the surface using a brush, spray gun, or roller; choosing the most appropriate tool for applying paint is one of the most important decisions a painter must make because using incorrect tools often slows down the work and produces unacceptable results. Spray guns are used generally for large surfaces or objects that do not lend themselves to brush work, such as lattices, cinder and concrete block, and radiators.

Many painters specialize in working on exterior surfaces only, painting house sidings and outside walls of large buildings. When doing work on tall buildings, scaffolding (raised supportive platforms) must be erected to allow the painter to climb to his or her position at various heights above the ground; workers also might use swinglike and chairlike platforms hung from heavy cables.

The first task of the paperhanger is similar to that of the painter: to prepare the surface to be covered. Rough spots must be smoothed, holes and cracks must be filled, and old paint, varnish, and grease must be removed from the surface. In some cases, old wallpaper must be removed by brushing it with solvent, soaking it down with water, or steaming it with portable steamer equipment. In new work, the paperhangers apply sizing, which is a prepared glazing material used as filler to make the plaster less porous and to ensure that the paper sticks well to the surface.

After erecting any necessary scaffolding, the paperhangers measure the area to be covered and cut the paper to size. They then mix paste and apply it to the back of the paper, which is then placed on the wall or ceiling and smoothed into place with brushes or rollers. In placing the paper on the wall, paperhangers must make sure that they match any design patterns at the adjacent edges of paper strips, cut overlapping ends, and smooth the seams between each strip.

Requirements

Basic skills requirements are the same for both painters and paperhangers. Most employers prefer to hire applicants in good physical condition, with manual dexterity (or the equivalent) and a good sense of color. Although a high school education is not essential, it is preferred that workers have at least the equivalent of a high school diploma (i.e., a GED). For protection of their own health, applicants should not be allergic to paint fumes or other materials used in the trade.

To qualify as a skilled painter or paperhanger, a person must also complete either an apprenticeship or an on-the-job training program. The apprenticeship program, which often combines painting and paperhanging, consists of three years of carefully planned activity, including work experience and related classroom instruction (approximately 144 hours of courses each year). During this period the apprentice becomes familiar with all aspects of the craft: use of tools and equipment, preparation of surfaces as well as of paints and pastes, application methods, coordination of colors, reading of blueprints, characteristics of wood and other surfaces, cost-estimating methods, and safety techniques. Courses often involve the study of mathematics as well as practice sessions on the techniques of the trade.

On-the-job training programs involve learning the trade informally while working for two to three years under the guidance of experienced painters or paperhangers. The trainees usually begin as helpers until they acquire the necessary skills and knowledge for more difficult jobs. Workers without formal apprenticeship training are more easily accepted in these crafts than in most of the other building trades.

Opportunities for Experience & Exploration

In high school and vocational school there are several ways to explore the skills of the painter and paperhanger. Courses in art, industrial arts, and wood shop will test students' interest and ability in this type of work, while courses in chemistry and mathematics will gauge their aptitude in the characteristics of materials (such as paints, varnishes, and pastes) and in cost estimation.

Other opportunities can be explored by reading trade journals and watching instructional videos or television programs. Those who already have some experience in the trade should keep up with the news by reading such publications as the monthly *Painters and Allied Trades Journal,* available to members of the painters and allied trades union. Look for educational videos at your local library, and check your TV listings for such programs as *This Old House.*

Certainly, painting and paperhanging in one's own home or apartment provides valuable firsthand experience, often impossible to obtain in other fields. Also valuable is the experience gained with a part-time or summer job as a helper to skilled workers who are already in the trade. Those who have done satisfactory part-time work sometimes go to work full time for the same employer after a certain period of time.

Methods of Entering

There are two ways that individuals can enter the painting and paperhanging trades: as apprentices or as on-the-job trainees. If they wish to become apprentices, the applicants usually contact employers (such as painting and paperhanging contractors), the state employment service bureau, the state apprenticeship agency, or the appropriate union headquarters (International Brotherhood of Painters and Allied Trades). They must, however, have the approval of the joint labor–management apprenticeship committee before they can enter the occupation by this method.

If the apprentice program is filled, applicants may wish to enter the trade as on-the-job trainees. In this case, they usually contact employers directly and begin work as helpers.

Advancement

Successful completion of one of the two types of training programs is necessary before individuals can become qualified, skilled painters or paperhangers. If workers have management ability and good planning skills, and if they work for a large contracting firm, they may advance to the following positions: supervisor, who supervises and coordinates activities of other workers; painting and decorating contract estimator, who computes material requirements and labor costs; and superintendent on a large contract painting job.

Some painters and paperhangers, once they have acquired enough capital and business experience, go into business for themselves as painting and decorating contractors. These self-employed workers must be able to take care of all standard business affairs, such as bookkeeping, insurance and legal matters, advertising, and billing.

Employment Outlook

In the early 1990s, there are about 465,000 painters and paperhangers employed in the United States; most of these workers are painters,and most are members of the trade union. About 40 percent of these workers are self-employed. Jobs are found mainly with contractors who work on projects such as new construction, remodeling, and restoration; others are found as maintenance workers for such establishments as schools, apartment complexes, and high-rise buildings.

Employment of painters and paperhangers is expected to grow faster than the average for all occupations through the next decade. Most job openings will occur as other workers retire, transfer, or otherwise leave the occupation. Turnover is very high in this trade. Openings for paperhangers will be fewer than those for painters, however, because this is a smaller specialized trade.

Increased construction will generate a need for more painters to work on new buildings and industrial structures. However, this will also lead to increased competition among self-employed painters and painting contractors for the better jobs. Newer types of paint have made it easier for inexperienced persons to do their own painting, but this does not affect the employment outlook much because most painters and paperhangers work on industrial and commercial projects and are not dependent on residential work.

Earnings

Painters and paperhangers tend to earn more per hour than other workers, but their total annual incomes may be less because of work time lost due to poor weather and periods of layoffs between contract assignments. The average annual beginning salary for painters and paperhangers is about $12,000; for more experienced workers, $24,000; and for the top wage earners, $38,000. Wages often vary depending on the geographic location of the job. Apprentices tend to earn starting wages that are about 50 percent less than those of more experienced workers.

Conditions of Work

Most painters and paperhangers have a standard forty-hour workweek, and they usually earn extra pay for working overtime. Their work requires them to stand for long periods of time, to climb, and to bend. Painters work both indoors and out-

119

doors, because their job may entail painting interior surfaces as well as exterior siding and other areas; paperhangers work exclusively indoors.

Because these occupations involve working on ladders and often with electrical equipment such as power sanders and paint sprayers, workers must adhere to safety standards.

Sources of Additional Information

■ International Brotherhood of Painters and Allied Trades
United Nations Building
1750 New York Avenue, NW
Washington, DC 20006
Tel: 202-637-0700

■ National Association of Home Builders
15th and M Streets, NW
Washington, DC 20005
Tel: 202-822-0200

■ National Joint Painting, Decorating, and Drywall Apprenticeship and Training Committee
1750 New York Avenue, NW
Washington, DC 20006
Tel: 202-783-7770

■ Painting and Decorating Contractors of America
3913 Old Lee Highway, Suite 33B
Fairfax, VA 22030
Tel: 703-359-0826

Pipefitters and Steamfitters

School Subjects
Mathematics
Shop (Trade/Vo-tech education)

Personal Interests
Building things
Fixing things

Work Environment
Indoors and outdoors
Primarily multiple locations

Minimum Education Level
High school diploma
Apprenticeship

Salary Range
$9,000 to $38,000

Certification or Licensing
Recommended

Outlook
More slowly than the average

DOT: 862   **GOE:** 05.05.03   **NOC:** 7252

Definition

Pipefitters and *steamfitters* design, install, and maintain the piping systems for steam, hot water, heating, cooling, lubricating, sprinkling, and industrial processing systems.

History

The Industrial Revolution marked the emergence of pipefitting as an independent trade. Prior to this period, general plumbers handled the construction and maintenance of piping systems. Additionally, indoor plumbing and municipal water systems were not as widespread as they are today, so regular plumbers could handle the workload.

This all changed with the Industrial Revolution. Factories and other buildings were being erected, cities were expanding, and new homes

121

were being built. All this development called for more indoor plumbing. The expansion of industry also brought about new uses for piping, such as the conveyance of steam, oil, chemicals, heat, natural gas, and compressed air in manufacturing processes. All of this building and expansion required larger and more varied piping systems, and pipefitting gradually became a profession in its own right.

Nature of the Work

Pipe systems carry more than just water. In power plants, they carry live steam to the turbines to create electricity. At oil refineries, pipes carry raw crude oil to processing tanks, then transport the finished products, such as petroleum, kerosene, and natural gas, to storage areas. In some manufacturing plants, pneumatic (air) pipe systems are used to monitor and adjust the industrial processes in the plant. Naval ships, submarines, aircraft, food processing plants, refrigerated warehouses, nuclear power plants, and office buildings all depend heavily on pipe systems for their operation. Pipe systems are also needed in the home for natural gas, hot and cold water, and sewage.

Pipefitters are the tradespeople who design, install, and maintain all of these different pipe systems. Steamfitters construct pipe systems that must withstand high amounts of pressure. It is a skilled and demanding line of work, because careless or incomplete work could cost lives.

Pipefitters can work both in existing buildings and in buildings under construction. When working in an old building on a task such as installing a sprinkler system, a pipefitter (more appropriately, a *sprinkler fitter*) sometimes receives nothing more than a verbal description of the job to complete. The pipefitter then examines the blueprints of the building, makes the necessary measurements, and draws a layout for how the system is to be installed. Installing a new pipe system in an old building is trickier than in a new one because the system must adapt to the existing construction. Modifications made to accommodate the pipe system must not weaken the building's structure or interfere with its other operations. Pipefitters also frequently are called on to repair the pipes in old buildings.

When installing pipe systems in buildings under construction, the pipefitter usually works under the supervision of the general contractor for the project. The blueprints for the piping are usually drawn up by the architect and the contractor and show the type of piping needed, what kind of fixtures are required, and where valves and connectors should be placed.

Pipefitters and steamfitters work with pipes made of many different types of materials, including steel, cast iron, copper, lead, glass, and plastic. As they study the blueprints, the pipefitters decide what types of materials they will need and how much they will use. The first step in preparing the pipes is cutting them to the proper length. If pipes need to be screwed together, the pipefitter will cut threads into the ends of the pipe using a pipe threader, which is attached to the end of the pipe and rotated to cut a slowly spiralling groove into the pipe. To remove any metal burrs after the thread is cut, the pipefitter will clean it out using a pipe reamer. Pipes may also need to be bent to the proper angle, which is done with a bending device that can be either manually or electrically powered.

Once the pipes are sized and cut, they are put into position, and the pipefitter can determine what needs to be done to support or give access to the pipes. Occasionally, holes may need to be cut through ceilings, floors, or walls, or the pipes may need to be bracketed to ceiling joists or along walls. Then the pipes are fitted together. This may be done by screwing the pipes into couplers, elbow joints, connectors, or special valves. Very large pipes, such as sewer pipes, have flat flanges that are bolted together when joined. At this stage, the pipefitter installs special mechanisms such as pressure gauges or meters.

Finally, the connections between the pipes are sealed and made airtight. Depending on the material the pipe is made of, this is done by soldering, caulking, brazing, fusing, or cementing the joints of the pipes together. The pipe system is then tested to make certain it is completely sealed. Water, air, or gas is pumped into the system at a high pressure and leaks are checked either personally by the pipefitter or an apprentice, or mechanically by means of gauges attached to the pipes. Proper and complete sealing is extremely important. Leaks will affect the performance of the entire system, and in certain cases, such as high-pressure steam pipes or pipes carrying noxious chemicals, leaks can be deadly.

Requirements

Pipefitters and steamfitters learn their occupations through apprenticeship programs. These programs take five years to complete, combining on-the-job training with a minimum of 216 hours of related classroom instruction each year. To apply for apprenticeship programs, people must be at least eighteen years of age, be in good physical condition, and have earned a high school diploma or its equivalent. Apprentice applicants are expected to have taken high school courses in shop, drafting, mathematics, physics, chemistry, and blueprint reading. Coursework from vocational schools and correspondence schools can also supplement an apprentice's training. To measure their mechanical readiness for this profession, apprentice applicants also must take mechanical aptitude tests.

Apprentices sign a written agreement with the local apprenticeship committee, which is made up of members from both union and management. This committee sets the standards for work and training that ensure apprentices gain a broad range of experience through employment with several different contractors. In their training period, they learn to cut, bend, fit, solder, and weld pipes. They also learn the proper use and care of tools and equipment, materials handling, workplace operations and safety (including the regulations of the Occupational Safety and Health Administration), and how to make cost estimates.

Pipefitters and steamfitters also learn related construction techniques, such as installing gas furnaces, boilers, pumps, oil burners, and radiators. They study and work on various heating and cooling systems, hot water systems, and solar and radiant heat systems. They explore industrial applications such as pneumatic control systems and instrumentation. Classroom work for apprentices includes subjects such as drafting, blueprint reading, applied math and physics, and local building codes and regulations.

Union membership often is a requirement for most pipefitters and steamfitters. The main union representing this trade is the United Association of Journeymen and Apprentices of the Plumbing and Pipe Fitting Industry of the United States and Canada. In certain industries such as the aerospace or petroleum industries, pipefitters and steamfitters may belong to other unions as well.

In some cities, pipefitters, steamfitters, and sprinkler fitters must be licensed. This requires passing a written test that covers local building and plumbing codes and offering proof of training and skills in the trade.

Opportunities for Experience & Exploration

To get an idea of the type of work done by pipefitters and steamfitters, students can look for jobs as construction helpers to these trades. This does not involve the commitment of an apprenticeship, and it is a good vantage point from which to consider whether one is interested in the type of work pipefitters do and the amount of training that the profession requires. A job as a helper is also a very good stepping stone to apprenticeship programs.

Methods of Entering

After completing high school, those interested in a career as a pipefitter should seek out information on the various apprenticeship programs available. To do this, job seekers should visit the nearest plumbing and pipefitting union local or nearby construction contractors to learn the details of apprenticeship programs and how to apply.

Another source for this information is the state employment service office of the U.S. Department of Labor, Bureau of Apprenticeship and Training. Applicants may have to take an aptitude test for admittance to apprenticeship programs.

For those who do not want to commit to an apprenticeship program, local unions and contractors are the best sources for work. Both unions and contractors may hire helpers to pipefitters and steamfitters.

Advancement

After their training, apprentice pipefitters become journeyworkers, which means more money and more employment opportunities. They may continue to work for the same contractor or move on to a new employer. If they gain experience in all the skills of the trade, they may rise to the position of supervisor. Some pipefitters and steamfitters decide to go into business for themselves as independent contractors, lining up job contracts and hiring their own employees. According to the Department of Labor, one out of every seven pipefitters is self-employed.

Employment Outlook

Employment prospects are good for pipefitters, steamfitters, and sprinkler fitters in the next few years. According to the Department of Labor, about sixty-one thousand jobs will open during the 1990s, although the projected growth is more slowly than the average. Those pipefitters who work in construction can sometimes experience layoffs when there are lulls in construction activity, while those who maintain existing pipe systems have steadier work. Pipefitters and steamfitters are less sensitive to swings in the economy than other construction trades.

Expansion of certain industries, such chemical and food-processing factories and others that rely on automated production, will be an important source of work for pipefitters. In office and home construction, air-conditioning and refrigeration systems will keep pipefitters busy, as will legislation requiring sprinkler systems in older buildings. Keeping existing pipe systems in good repair will employ many workers in the trade.

Earnings

Although pay rates vary somewhat in different areas of the country, earnings for pipefitters and steamfitters are among the highest in the construction trades. Hourly rates for pipefitters range from $5.50 to $16.00 in the southwestern United States. Steamfitters earn monthly wages ranging from $1,680 to $3,175. Union plumbers, pipefitters, and steamfitters earn an average weekly wage of $789 in the 1990s. Sprinkler fitters have an annual median salary of $34,700 in the 1990s.

Apprentices typically earn from 30 to 50 percent of a journeyworker's wage at the beginning of their training. If their work remains satisfactory, their wages are raised at regular intervals, usually six months, as stipulated in their apprenticeship agreements. Those applicants with some relevant training or experience may receive a higher wage when they begin their apprenticeship. Pipefitters and steamfitters also enjoy a variety of benefits from their employer or union, including health insurance, pension plans, paid vacations, and training opportunities.

Conditions of Work

Like other construction and maintenance work, pipefitting is hard, dirty, and active work. Much of their work is done in cramped quarters and in uncomfortable positions. Lifting, joining, and installing heavy pipe work and operating large machinery can cause fatigue and muscle strain. Other hazards include cuts from sharp tools, burns from hot pipes and welding material, and related construction injuries. However, the injury rate for pipefitters and steamfitters is the same as the average for most construction employees.

Most pipefitters and steamfitters are employed by building contractors and perform their work at different sites every day. They may work for a few hours at one work site and then travel to another. However, the construction of a large housing or industrial complex may keep pipefitters at the same site for several months. Pipefitters work a regular forty-hour week, although they may work overtime to meet deadlines or complete assignments. Pipefitters on the maintenance staff of a large processing plant generally work from thirty-five to forty hours a week.

Pipefitting, steamfitting, and sprinkler fitting are demanding trades. Aside from the physical strain the work requires, pipefitters must also perform very careful, conscientious, and exacting work. Flaws in their work could lead to damage to property and injury to others. They must be able not only to follow instructions, but also to apply judgment and experience to make decisions and direct other workers when necessary.

Pipefitters and steamfitters invest a lot of time into their training for the profession, so relatively few of them leave the field to move into other lines of work. Work is usually available in every part of the country, and the pay is above average. Pipefitters and steamfitters also enjoy the satisfaction of working in one of the skilled construction trades.

Sources of Additional Information

■ **Mechanical Contractors Association of America**
1385 Piccard Drive
Rockville, MD 20850
Tel: 301-869-5800

■ **National Association of Plumbing-Heating-Cooling Contractors**
PO Box 6808
180 South Washington Street
Falls Church, VA 22040
Tel: 703-237-8100

Plasterers

School Subjects
Art
Shop (Trade/Vo-tech education)

Personal Interests
Construction
Drawing/painting

Work Environment
Primarily indoors
Primarily multiple locations

Minimum Education Level
High school diploma
Apprenticeship

Salary Range
$17,772 to $39,180

Certification or Licensing
None

Outlook
Little change or more slowly than the average

DOT: 840   **GOE:** 05.05.04   **NOC:** 7284

Definition

Plasterers apply coats of plaster to interior walls, ceilings, and partitions of buildings to produce fire-resistant and relatively soundproof surfaces. They also work on exterior building surfaces or do ornamental forming and casting work. Their work is similar to that of *drywall workers,* who use drywall rather than plaster to build interior walls and ceilings.

History

Plastering is one of the most ancient crafts in the building trades. Before current plasters were invented, primitive people used damp clay, sand, grasses, or reeds. They used their hands, stones, and early tools to smooth the surfaces of the walls of their dwellings. The trade has evolved into a highly skilled type of work through the development and use of many new and improved materials and techniques.

Nature of the Work

Plasterers work on building interiors and exteriors. They apply plaster directly to masonry, wire, wood, metal or lath. (Lath is a supportive reinforcement made of wood or metal that is attached to studs to form walls and ceilings.) These surfaces are all designed to hold the plaster in position until it dries. After checking the specifications and plans made by the builder, architect, or foreman, plasterers begin by putting a border of plaster of the desired thickness on the top and bottom of the wall. After this border has hardened sufficiently, they fill in the remaining portion of the wall with two coats of plaster. The surface of the wall area is then leveled and smoothed with a straight-edged tool and a darby (a long flat tool used for smoothing). They then apply the third or finishing coat of plaster, which is the last operation before painting or paperhanging. This coat may be finished to an almost velvet smoothness or into one of a variety of decorative textures that are used in place of papering.

When plastering cinder block and concrete, plasterers first apply what is known as a brown coat of gypsum plaster as a base. The second coat, called the white coat, is lime-based plaster. When plastering metal lath foundations, they first apply a scratch coat with a trowel, spread it over the lath, and scratch the surface with a rake-like tool to make ridges before it dries so that the next coat—the brown coat—will bond tightly. Next, the plasterer sprays or trowels the plaster for the brown coat and smoothes it. The finishing coat is either sprayed on or applied with a hawk and trowel. Plasterers also use brushes and water for the finishing coat. The final coat is a mix of lime, water, and plaster of Paris that sets quickly and is smooth and durable.

The plasterer sometimes works with plasterboard or sheetrock, types of wallboard that come ready for installation. When working with such wallboard, the plasterer cuts and fits the wallboard to the studding and joists of ceilings and interior walls. When installing ceilings, workers perform as a team.

Plasterers who specialize in exterior plastering are known as stucco masons. They apply a weather-resistant decorative covering of portland cement plaster to lath in the same manner as interior plastering or with the use of a spray gun. In exterior work, however, the finish coat usually consists of a mixture of white cement and sand, or a patented finish material that may be applied in a variety of colors and textures.

Decorative and ornamental plastering is the specialty of highly skilled molding plasterers. This work includes molding or forming and installing ornamental plaster panels and trim. Some molding plasterers also cast intricate cornices and the recesses used for indirect lighting. Such work is rarely used today because of the great degree of skill involved and the high cost.

In recent years, most plasterers use machines to spray plaster on walls, ceilings, and structural sections of buildings. Machines that mix plaster have been in general use for many years.

Requirements

Most employers prefer to hire applicants who are at least seventeen years old, in good physical condition, and who have a high degree of manual dexterity. Although a high school or trade school education is not mandatory, it is highly recommended. To qualify as a journeyman plasterer, a person must complete either an apprenticeship or an on-the-job training program.

The apprenticeship program consists of three to four years of carefully planned activity combining from about 6,000 to about 8,000 hours of work experience with an annual 144 hours of related classroom instruction. An apprenticeship is usually the best start, since it includes on-the-job training as well as supervision.

On-the-job training consists of working for four or more years under the supervision of experienced plasterers. The trainee usually begins as a helper or laborer and learns the trade informally by observing or by being taught by other plasterers.

Opportunities for Experience & Exploration

In high school or vocational school, students have several avenues open for exploring the occupation of plasterer. Mechanical drawing, drafting, woodwork, and other shop courses will test their ability and aptitude for this type of work, while courses in mathematics will gauge their skill in the applied mathematics of layout work.

To observe the plasterer at work, field trips to construction sites can be arranged by a school counselor, or students can arrange an interview on their own.

An excellent firsthand experience in this trade would be to obtain a part-time or summer job as a plasterer's helper or laborer.

Methods of Entering

There are two ways individuals can enter this field: as apprentices or as on-the-job trainees. Those who wish to become apprentices usually contact local plastering contractors, the state employment service bureau, or the appropriate union headquarters. In most places, the local branch of the Operative Plasterers' and Cement Masons' International Association of the United States and Canada is the best place to inquire about apprenticeships. The Bureau of Apprenticeship and Training, U.S. Department of Labor, and the state employment office are also good places to contact for information.

If the apprenticeship program is filled, applicants may wish to enter the field as on-the-job trainees. In this case, they usually contact a plastering contractor directly and begin work as helpers or laborers. They learn about the work by mixing the plaster, helping plasterers with scaffolding, and carrying equipment.

Advancement

Successful completion of a training program is necessary before individuals can become qualified plasterers. It takes four years to become proficient in most plastering techniques. After increasing their skill and efficiency for a few years, several promotional opportunities are open to them.

Most plasterers learn the full range of plastering skills. They develop expertise in finish plastering as well as rough coat plastering. They also learn the spray gun technique and become proficient spray gun plasterers. With additional training, they may specialize in exterior work as stucco masons or in ornamental plastering as molding plasterers.

If they have certain personal characteristics such as the ability to deal with people, good judgment, and planning skills, plasterers may progress to become supervisors or job estimators. Many plasterers become self-employed, and some eventually become contractors.

Employment Outlook

There are approximately thirty-two thousand plasterers employed in the United States in the 1990s. Employment opportunities for plasterers are expected to increase slowly during the remainder of the decade and beyond, because of the trend toward wider use of drywall construction. Plasterers' employment prospects usually rise and fall with the economy, and especially with the health of the construction industry.

However, recent improvements in both plastering materials and methods of application are expected to increase the scope of the craft and create more job opportunities. To name a few such developments: more lightweight plasters are being used because of excellent soundproofing, acoustical, and fireproofing qualities; machine plastering, insulating, and fireproofing are becoming more widespread; and the use of plaster veneer or high-density plaster in creating a finished surface is being used increasingly in new buildings. Plaster veneer is a thin coat of plaster that can be finished in one coat. It is made of lime and plaster of Paris and can be mixed with water at the job site. It is often applied to a special gypsum base on interior surfaces. Exterior systems have also changed to include Styrofoam insulation board and two thin coats of polymer and acrylic modified materials, called Exterior Insulated Finish Systems, or EIFS.

Earnings

The median annual salary for plasterers in the 1990s was about $29,300. However, the minimum wage rate varied considerably according to the section of the country. Hourly wages varied from lows of $4.50 and $5.00 to $23.00 for experienced plasterers in certain communities. Average monthly wages ranged from $1,481 to $3,265. Plasterers can also receive traditional fringe benefits, such as health insurance.

Conditions of Work

Most plasterers have a regular forty-hour workweek, with occasional overtime when it is necessary to meet a contract deadline. Overtime work is compensated at the rate of one and a half times the regular hourly wage. The workday may start earlier than most (7:00 AM), but it also usually ends earlier (3:00 PM). Some plasterers face layoffs between jobs, while others may work with drywall or ceiling tile as required by their contractors when there is no plastering work to be done.

Most of the work is performed indoors, plastering walls, ceilings, and forming and casting ornamental designs. Plasterers also work outdoors, doing stucco work and EIFS. They often work with other construction people, including carpenters, plumbers, and pipefitters. Plasterers must do a considerable amount of standing, stooping, and lifting. They often get plaster on their work clothes and dust in their eyes and noses.

132

Most plasterers work for independent contractors and are members of unions, either the Operative Plasterers' and Cement Masons' International Association of the United States and Canada or the International Union of Bricklayers and Allied Craftsmen.

Plasterers can take pride in seeing the results of their work—something they have helped to build that will last a long time. Their satisfaction with progress on the job, day by day, may be a great deal more than in those jobs where the worker never sees the completed work or where the results are not so obvious.

As highly skilled workers, plasterers have higher earnings, better chances for promotion, and more opportunity to go into business for themselves than other workers. They also can usually find jobs in almost any part of the United States.

Sources of Additional Information

■ **Foundation of the Wall and Ceiling Industry**
307 East Annandale Road, Suite 200
Falls Church, VA 22042
Tel: 703-534-1703

■ **International Institute for Lath and Plaster**
820 Transfer Road
St. Paul, MN 55114
Tel: 612-645-0208

■ **International Union of Bricklayers and Allied Craftsmen**
815 15th Street, NW
Washington, DC 20005
Tel: 202-783-3788

■ **Operative Plasterers' and Cement Masons' International Association of the United States and Canada**
1125 17th Street, NW
Washington, DC 20036
Tel: 202-393-6569

■ **Mason Contractors of America**
1550 Spring Road, Suite 320
Oak Brook, IL 60521
Tel: 630-782-6767

Plumbers

School Subjects
Chemistry
Physics

Personal Interests
Building things
Finding out how things work

Work Environment
Primarily indoors
Primarily multiple locations

Minimum Education Level
High school diploma
Apprenticeship

Salary Range
$19,740 to $38,868

Certification or Licensing
Required in most states

Outlook
As fast as the average

DOT: 862   **GOE:** 05.05.03   **NOC:** 7251

Definition

Plumbers assemble, install, alter, and repair pipes and pipe systems that carry water, steam, air, or other liquids and gases for sanitation and industrial purposes as well as other uses. Plumbers also install plumbing fixtures, appliances, and heating and refrigerating units.

History

Although the early Egyptians are known to have used lead pipes to carry water and drainage into and out of buildings, the use of plumbing in a citywide system was first achieved in the Roman Empire.

In Renaissance times, the techniques of plumbing were revived and used in some of the great castles and monasteries. But, the greatest advances in plumbing, though, were made in the nineteenth century, when towns grew into cities and the need for adequate public sanitation was recognized.

Nature of the Work

Because little difference exists between the work of the plumber and the *pipefitter* in most cases, the two are often considered to be one trade. However, many craft workers specialize in one field or the other, especially in large cities.

The work of pipefitters differs from that of plumbers mainly in its location and in the variety and size of the pipes used. Plumbers work primarily in residential and commercial buildings, whereas pipefitters are generally employed by a large industry such as an oil refinery, refrigeration plant, or defense establishment where more complex systems of piping are used. Plumbers assemble, install, and repair heating, water, and drainage systems, especially those that must be connected to public utility systems. Some of their jobs include replacing burst pipes and installing and repairing sinks, bathtubs, water heaters, hot water tanks, garbage disposal units, dishwashers, and water softeners. Plumbers may also work on septic tanks, cesspools, and sewers. During the final construction stages of both commercial and residential buildings, plumbers install heating and air-conditioning units and connect radiators, water heaters, and plumbing fixtures.

Most plumbers follow set procedures in their work. After inspecting the installation site to determine pipe location, they cut and thread pipes, bend them to required angles by hand or with machines, and then join them by means of welded, brazed, caulked, soldered, or threaded joints. To test for leaks in the system, they fill the pipes with water or air.

Specialists include *diesel engine pipe fitters, ship and boat building coppersmiths, industrial-gas fitters, gas-main fitters, prefab plumbers,* and *pipe cutters.*

Plumbers use a variety of tools, including hand tools such as wrenches, reamers, drills, braces and bits, hammers, chisels, and saws; power machines that cut, bend, and thread pipes; gasoline torches; and welding, soldering, and brazing equipment.

Requirements

Most employers prefer to hire applicants who are at least eighteen years old, in good physical condition, and with a high degree of mechanical aptitude. Although a high school education is not required, it is generally preferred. The student's preparation should include courses in mathematics, chemistry, and physics, as well as some shop courses.

To qualify as a plumber, a person must complete either a formal apprenticeship or an informal on-the-job training program. To be considered for the apprenticeship program, individuals must pass an examination administered by the state employment agency and have their qualifications approved by the local joint labor–management apprenticeship committee.

The apprenticeship program for plumbers consists of four years of carefully planned activity combining direct training with at least 144 hours of formal classroom instruction each year. The program is designed to give apprentices diversified training by having them work for several different plumbing or pipefitting contractors.

On-the-job training, on the other hand, usually consists of working for five or more years under the guidance of an experienced craft worker. The trainees begin as helpers until they acquire the necessary skills and knowledge for more difficult jobs. Frequently, they must supplement this practical training by taking trade- or correspondence-school courses.

A license is required for plumbers in many places. To obtain this license, plumbers must pass a special examination to demonstrate their knowledge of local building codes as well as their all-around knowledge of the trade. To become a plumbing contractor in most places, a master plumber's license must be obtained.

Opportunities for Experience & Exploration

Although opportunities for direct experience in this occupation are rare for those in high school, there are ways to explore the field. Courses in chemistry, physics, mechanical drawing, and mathematics are all helpful to the work of the plumber and pipefitter. By taking these courses in high school, students will test their ability and aptitude in the theoretical aspects of the trade.

Methods of Entering

Applicants who wish to become apprentices usually contact local plumbing, heating, and air-conditioning contractors who employ plumbers, the state employment service bureau, or the local branch of the United Association of Journeymen and Apprentices of the Plumbing and Pipe Fitting Industry of the United States and Canada. Individual contractors or contractor associations often sponsor local apprenticeship programs. Before becoming apprentices, however, prospective plumbers must have the approval of the joint labor–management apprenticeship committee. Both union and nonunion apprenticeships typically last four to five years. The Bureau of Apprenticeship and Training, the U.S. Department of Labor, and state employment offices are also good places to contact for information.

If applicants are rejected from apprenticeship programs or if the programs are filled, they may wish to enter the field as on-the-job trainees. Others pursue plumbing training through the armed forces.

Advancement

Successful completion of a training program is necessary before an individual can become a qualified journeyman plumber, and licenses are required in most communities. It takes two to four years to master most of the skills the plumber needs to perform everyday tasks.

If plumbers have certain qualities, such as the ability to deal with people, good judgment, and planning skills, they may progress to such positions as supervisor or job estimator for plumbing or pipefitting contractors; or, if they work for a large industrial company, they may advance to the position of job superintendent.

Many plumbers go into business for themselves. Eventually they may expand their activities and become contractors, employing other workers.

Employment Outlook

Approximately three hundred thousand plumbers are employed during the 1990s. Employment opportunities for plumbers are expected to increase as fast as the average for all jobs through 2005. There are several reasons for this outlook. First and most important is the anticipated increase in construction activity. Second, plumbing and heating work in new homes is expected to include the installation of sprinkler systems, more bathrooms per house, washing machines, waste disposals, air-conditioning equipment, and solar heating devices. Third, because pipework is becoming more important in large industries, more workers will be needed for installation and maintenance work, especially where refrigeration and air-conditioning equipment are used. Fourth, the need to replace those who leave the field will provide thousands of job openings each year.

Earnings

The annual median salary for non–self-employed plumbers in the 1990s is $28,900. Wages vary, however, according to location. Monthly wages for plumbers range from $1,645 to $3,239. Hourly pay rates for apprentices usually start at 50 percent of the experienced worker's rate and increase by 5 percent every six months until a rate of 95 percent is reached. Benefits for union workers usually include health insurance, sick time, and vacation pay, as well as pension plans.

Conditions of Work

Most plumbers have a regular forty-hour workweek with extra pay for overtime. Unlike most of the other building trades, this field is little affected by seasonal factors.

The work of the plumber is active and strenuous. Standing for prolonged periods and working in cramped or uncomfortable positions are often necessary. Possible risks include falls from ladders, cuts from sharp tools, and burns from hot pipes or steam. Working with clogged pipes and toilets can also be smelly.

Those who would be successful and contented plumbers should like to solve a variety of problems and should not object to being called on during evenings, weekends, or holidays to perform emergency repairs. As in most service occupations, plumbers should be able to get along well with all kinds of people. The plumber should be a person who works well alone, but who can also direct the work of helpers and enjoy the company of those in the other construction trades.

Sources of Additional Information

■ **National Association of Plumbing-Heating-Cooling Contractors**
PO Box 6808
180 South Washington Street
Falls Church, VA 22040
Tel: 703-237-8100

■ **United Association of Journeymen and Apprentices of the Plumbing and Pipe Fitting Industry of the United States and Canada**
PO Box 37800
Washington, DC 20013
Tel: 202-628-5823

Roofers

School Subjects
Mathematics
Shop (Trade/Vo-tech education)

Personal Interests
Building things
Fixing things

Work Environment
Primarily outdoors
Primarily multiple locations

Minimum Education Level
High school diploma
Apprenticeship

Salary Range
$18,000 to $40,000

Certification or Licensing
Required for certain positions

Outlook
As fast as the average

DOT: 866   **GOE:** 04.10.01   **NOC:** 7291

Definition

Roofers install and repair roofs of buildings using a variety of materials and methods, including built-up roofing, single-ply roofing systems, asphalt shingles, tile, and slate. They may also waterproof and damp-proof walls, swimming pools, and other building surfaces.

History

Roofs have always been needed to cover buildings to protect their interiors against snow, rain, wind, temperature extremes, and strong sunlight. The earliest roofs were probably thatched with plant materials such as leaves, branches, or straw. Especially with clay or a similar substance pressed into any open spaces, such a roof can provide good protection from the weather. Roofs constructed on frameworks of thick branches or timbers allowed different roof designs to develop, including the flat and pitched, or sloping, forms that are in use today. When brick and stone began to be used in building, it became possible to construct domes and vaults, roof forms based on arches.

Throughout most of history, flat roofs have been associated with dry climates, where drainage of water off the roof is seldom a concern. In the nineteenth century, new roofing and building materials made flat roofs an economical alternative to pitched roofs in somewhat wetter conditions, such as those in much of the United States. Today, flat or very slightly sloped roofs are common on commercial buildings and are also used on some residential buildings. Pitched roofs in various forms have been used for many centuries, largely in climates where drainage is a concern. Most houses have pitched roofs.

All roofs must keep out water. There are two basic types of roof covering that do this: separate shingles, or flat pieces of a waterproof material that are placed so that water cannot get through at the joints; and a continuous layer or sheet membrane of a material that is impermeable to water. Different kinds of roofing materials are appropriate for different kinds of roofs, and each material has its own method of application.

The occupation of roofer has developed along with the various kinds of modern roofing materials. Roofers today must know about how the elements in each roofing system are used and how water, temperature, and humidity affect the roof. While asphalt shingle roofs on homes may require only relatively simple materials and application procedures, large commercial building roofs can involve complex preparation and layering of materials to produce the necessary protective covering.

Nature of the Work

Although roofers usually are trained to apply most kinds of roofing, they often specialize in either sheet membrane roofing or in prepared roofings such as asphalt shingles, slate, or tile.

One kind of sheet membrane roofing is called "built-up roofing." Built-up roofing, used on flat roofs, consists of roofing felt (fabric saturated in bitumen, a tar like material) laid into hot bitumen. To prepare for putting on a built-up roof, roofers may apply a layer of insulation to the bare roof deck. Then they spread molten bitumen all over the roof surface; lay down overlapping layers of roofing felt; and spread more hot bitumen over the felt, sealing the seams and making the roof watertight. They may repeat this process several times to build up as many layers as desired. They may give the top a smooth finish or embed gravel in the top for a rough surface.

Single-ply roofing is a relatively new method of roofing using a waterproof sheet membrane. Single-ply roofing, which is an increasing share of roofing work, employs any of several different types of chemical products. Some roofing consists of bituminous compounds that are rolled out in sheets on the building's insulation. The compound may be remelted on the roof by torch or hot anvil to fuse it to or embed it in hot bitumen in a manner similar to built-up roofing. Other single-ply roofing is made of rubber or plastic materials that can be sealed with contact adhesive cements, solvent welding, hot-air welding, or other methods. Still another type of single-ply roofing consists of spray-in-place polyurethane foam with a polymeric coating. Roofers who apply these roofing systems must be trained in the application methods for each system. Many manufacturers of these systems require that roofers take special courses and receive certification before they are authorized to use the products.

To apply asphalt shingles, a very common roofing on houses, roofers begin by cutting strips of roofing felt and tacking them down over the entire roof. They nail on horizontal rows of shingles, beginning at the low edge of the roof and working up. Sometimes they must cut shingles to fit around corners, vent pipes, and chimneys. Where two sections of roof meet, they nail or cement flashing, which is strips of metal or shingle that make the joints watertight.

Tile and slate shingles, which are more expensive types of residential roofing, are installed slightly differently. First, roofing felt is applied over the wood base. Next, the roofers punch holes in the slate or tile pieces so that nails can be inserted, or they embed the tiles in mortar. Each row of shingles overlaps the preceding row.

Metal roofing is applied by specially trained roofers or by *sheet metal workers*. One type of metal roof uses metal sections shaped like flat pans, soldered together for weather-proofing and attached by metal clips to the wood below. Another kind of metal roofing, called "standing seam roofing," has raised seams where the sections of sheet metal interlock.

Some roofers waterproof and damp-proof walls, swimming pools, tanks, and structures other than roofs. To prepare surfaces for waterproofing, workers smooth the very rough surfaces and roughen the glazed surfaces. They brush or spray waterproofing material on the surface. Damp-proofing is done by spraying a coating of tar or asphalt onto interior or exterior surfaces to prevent moisture from penetrating.

Various hand tools are used by roofers in their work, including hammers, roofing knives, mops, pincers, caulking guns, rollers, welders, chalk lines, and cutters.

Requirements

Most employers prefer to hire applicants at least eighteen years of age, in good physical condition, with a good sense of balance. Although a high school education or its equivalent is not required, it is preferred in most cases.

Roofers learn the skills they need through on-the-job training or by completing an apprenticeship. Most roofers learn informally on the job while they work under the supervision of experienced roofers. Beginners start out as helpers, doing simple tasks like carrying equipment and putting up scaffolding. They gradually gain the skills and knowledge they need for more difficult tasks. Roofers may need four or more years of on-the-job training to become familiar with all the materials and techniques they need to know.

Apprenticeship programs generally provide more thorough, balanced training. Apprenticeships are three years in length and combine a planned program of work experience with formal classroom instruction in related subjects. The work portion of the apprenticeship includes a minimum of 1,400 hours each year under the guidance of experienced roofers. The classroom instruction, at least 144 hours per year, covers such topics as safety practices, how to use and care for tools, and arithmetic.

Some roofers are members of The United Union of Roofers, Waterproofers and Allied Workers.

Opportunities for Experience & Exploration

High school or vocational school students may be able to get firsthand experience of this occupation through a part-time or summer job as a roofer's helper. Students can also take courses that familiarize them with some of the skills that are a regular part of roofing work. Courses that would be beneficial include shop, basic mathematics, and mechanical drawing.

It may be possible to visit a construction site to observe roofers at work, but a close look is unlikely, because roofers do most of their work at heights.

Methods of Entering

People who are planning to start out as helpers and learn on the job can contact roofing contractors directly to inquire about possible openings. Job leads may also be located through the local office of the state employment service or newspaper classified ads. Graduates of vocational schools may get useful information from the placement office of the school they attended.

People who want to become apprentices can find more about apprenticeships in their area by contacting local roofing contractors, the state employment service, or the local office of The United Union of Roofers, Waterproofers and Allied Workers.

Advancement

After gaining experience, roofers who work for roofing contractors may be promoted to supervisory positions in which they are responsible for coordinating the activities of other roofers. Another possibility may be to become an estimator, figuring the costs of doing roofing jobs before the work is done. Roofers who have the right combination of personal characteristics, including the ability to deal with people, good judgment, and planning skills, may be able to go into business for themselves as independent roofing contractors.

Employment Outlook

There are about 140,000 people employed as roofers in the United States. Over the next ten to fifteen years, employment in this field is expected to increase at about the same rate as the average for all occupations.

There are several reasons for this outlook. Roofers will continue to be in demand for the construction of new buildings. Furthermore, roofs tend to need more maintenance and repair work than other parts of buildings. The majority of roofing work is on existing structures. Roofers will always be needed for roof repairs and replacement, even during economic downturns when construction activity generally decreases. Also, damp-proofing and waterproofing are expected to provide an increasing proportion of the work done by roofers.

Every year, many openings will become available as people in the field transfer to other work, retire, or die. Because most roofing work is done during the warmer part of the year, job opportunities will probably be best during spring and summer.

Earnings

The earnings of roofers vary widely depending on how much time they work, their geographical location, their skills and experience, and other factors. Roofers average about thirty-three hours per week. Sometimes bad weather prevents them from working, and some weeks they work fewer than twenty hours. They make up for lost time in other weeks, and if they work longer hours than the standard workweek (usually about forty hours), they receive extra pay for the overtime. While roofers in northern states might not work in the winter, most roofers work year-round.

The average hourly wage for roofers is $13, with weekly earnings at about $430 and annual earnings at about $20,000. Some workers make less, and a few make nearly twice as much. Skilled and experienced roofers may earn $600 or more per week (about $28,000 annually). Annual earnings may not reflect hourly figures because layoffs in bad weather limit the number of hours roofers work.

Hourly wage rates for apprentices usually start at about 55 percent of the skilled worker's rate and increase periodically until the pay reaches 90 percent of the full rate during the final six months.

Conditions of Work

Roofers must be outdoors most of the time while they are on the job. They work in the heat and cold, but not in wet weather. Roofs can get extremely hot during the summer. The work is physically strenuous, involving lifting heavy weights, prolonged standing, climbing, bending, and squatting. Roofers must work while standing on surfaces that may be steep and quite high; they must use caution to avoid injuries from falls while working on ladders, scaffolding, or roofs.

Sources of Additional Information

- **National Roofing Contractors Association**
  10255 West Higgins Road, Suite 600
  Rosemont, IL 60018-5607
  Tel: 847-299-9070

- **Roofing Industry Educational Institute**
  14 Inverness Drive East
  Building H, Suite 110
  Englewood, CO 80112-5608
  Email: richroof@eworld.com

- **The United Union of Roofers, Waterproofers and Allied Workers**
  1660 L Street
  Washington, DC 20036

Sheet Metal Workers

School Subjects
Mathematics
Physics

Personal Interests
Model building
Sculpting

Work Environment
Primarily indoors
Primarily multiple locations

Minimum Education Level
High school diploma
Apprenticeship

Salary Range
$20,000 to $50,000

Certification or Licensing
None

Outlook
About as fast as the average

DOT: 804   **GOE:** 05.05.06   **NOC:** 7261

Definition

Sheet metal workers fabricate, assemble, install, repair, and maintain ducts used for ventilating, air-conditioning, and heating systems. They also work with other articles of sheet metal, including roofing, siding, gutters, downspouts, partitions, chutes, and stainless steel kitchen and beverage equipment for restaurants. Not included in this group are employees in factories where sheet metal items are mass-produced on assembly lines.

History

Not until the development of mills and processes that form various kinds of metal into thin, strong, flat sheets and strips did sheet metal became important in many products. The processes for making sheet metal have undergone a long series of improvements in the twentieth century. As the methods were refined and made more economical, new uses for sheet metal were developed, and making sheet metal products became a well-established skilled craft field. Today, sheet metal workers are concerned with cutting, shaping, soldering, riveting, and other processes to fabricate, install, and maintain a wide range of articles. Heating, ventilating, and air-conditioning systems for all kinds of buildings—residential, commercial, industrial—provide the most important source of employment for sheet metal workers.

Nature of the Work

Most sheet metal workers handle a variety of tasks in fabricating, installing, and maintaining sheet metal products. Some workers concentrate on just one of these areas. Skilled workers must know about the whole range of activities involved in working with sheet metal.

Many sheet metal workers are employed by building contracting firms that construct or renovate residential, commercial, and industrial buildings. Fabricating and installing air-conditioning, heating, and refrigeration equipment is often a big part of their job. Some workers specialize in adjusting and servicing equipment that has already been installed so that it can operate at peak efficiency. Roofing contractors, the federal government, and businesses that do their own alteration and construction work also employ sheet metal workers. Other sheet metal workers are employed in the shipbuilding, railroad, and aircraft industries or in shops that manufacture specialty products like custom kitchen equipment or electrical generating and distributing machinery.

Fabricating is often done in a shop away from the site where the product is to be installed. In fabricating products, workers usually begin by studying blueprints or drawings. After determining the amount and kind of materials required for the job, they make measurements and lay out the work on the appropriate kinds of metal. They may use measuring tapes and rulers and figure dimensions with the aid of calculators. Then, following the pattern they have marked on the metal, they cut out the sections with hand or power shears or other machine tools. They may shape the pieces with a hand or machine brake, which is a type of equipment used for bending and forming sheet metal. They may punch or drill holes in the parts. As a last step before assembly, workers inspect the parts to verify that all of them are accurately shaped. Then they fasten the parts together by welding, soldering, bolting, riveting, or cementing them, or by using special devices such as metal clips. After assembly, it may be necessary to smooth rough areas on the fabricated item with a file or grinding wheel.

Computers play an increasingly important role in several of these tasks. Computers help workers plan the layout efficiently, so that all the necessary sections can be cut from the metal stock while leaving the smallest possible amount of leftover waste sheet metal. Computers also help guide saws, shears, and even lasers that cut metal, as well as other machines that form the pieces into the desired shapes.

If the item has been fabricated in a shop, it is taken to the installation site. There, the sheet metal workers may join together different sections of the final product. For example, they may connect sections of duct end to end. Some items, such as sections of duct, can be bought factory-made in standard sizes, and workers modify them at the installation site to meet the requirements of the situation. Once finished, duct work may be suspended with metal hangers from ceilings or attached to walls. Sometimes sheet metal workers weld, bolt, screw, or nail items into place. To complete the installation, they may need to make additional sheet metal parts or alter the items they have fabricated.

Some tasks in working with sheet metal, such as making metal roofing, are routinely done at the job site. Workers measure and cut sections of roof paneling, which interlock with grooving at the edges. They nail or weld the paneling to the roof deck to hold it in place and put metal molding over joints and around the edges, windows, and doors to finish off the roof.

Requirements

The best way to learn the skills necessary for working in this field is to complete an apprenticeship. Apprenticeships generally consist of a planned series of on-the-job work experiences plus classroom instruction in related subjects. The on-the-job training portion of apprenticeships, which last at least four years, includes about eight thousand hours of work. The classroom instruction totals approximately six hundred hours, spread over the years of the apprenticeship. The training covers all aspects of sheet metal fabrication and installation.

Apprentices get practical experience in layout work, cutting, shaping, and installing sheet metal. They also learn to work with materials that are sometimes used instead of metal, such as fiberglass and plastics. Under the supervision of skilled workers, they begin with simple tasks and gradually work up to the most complex. In the classroom, they learn blueprint reading, drafting, mathematics, computer operations, job safety, welding, and the principles of heating, air-conditioning, and ventilating systems.

Apprenticeships may be run by joint committees representing locals of the Sheet Metal Workers' International Association, an important union in the field, and local chapters of the Sheet Metal and Air Conditioning Contractors' National Association. Other apprenticeships are run by local chapters of a contractor group, the Associated Builders and Contractors. Requirements vary slightly, but usually applicants for apprenticeships must be high school graduates. High school courses that would be part of a good background include shop classes, mechanical drawing, trigonometry, and geometry. Applicants need to be in good physical condition, with good manual dexterity, eye-hand coordination, and the ability to visualize and understand shapes and forms.

A few sheet metal workers learn informally on the job while they are employed as helpers to experienced workers. They gradually pick up skills when opportunities arise for learning. Like apprentices, helpers start out with simple jobs and in time take on more complicated work. However, the training that helpers get may not be as balanced, and it may take longer for them to learn all that they need to know. Helpers often take vocational school courses to supplement their work experience.

Even after they have become experienced and well qualified in their field, sheet metal workers may need to take further training to keep their skills up to date. Such training is often sponsored by union groups or paid for by their employers.

Opportunities for Experience & Exploration

High school students can gauge their aptitude for and interest in some of the common activities of sheet metal workers by taking courses such as metal shop, blueprint reading, and mechanical drawing. A summer or part-time job as a helper with a contracting firm that does sheet metal work could provide an excellent opportunity to observe workers on the job. If such a job cannot be arranged, it may be possible to visit a construction site and perhaps to talk with a sheet metal worker who can give an insider's view of this job.

Methods of Entering

People who would like to enter an apprentice program in this field can seek information about apprenticeships from local employers of sheet metal workers, such as sheet metal contractors or heating, air-conditioning, and refrigeration contractors; from the local office of the Sheet Metal Workers' International Association; or from the local Sheet Metal Apprentice Training office, the joint union–management apprenticeship committee. Information on apprenticeship programs may also be obtained from the local office of the state employment service or the state apprenticeship agency.

People who would rather enter this field as on-the-job trainees can contact contractors directly about possibilities for jobs as helpers. Leads for specific jobs may also be located through the state employment service or newspaper classified ads. Graduates of vocational or technical training programs may get assistance from the placement office at their school.

Advancement

Skilled and experienced sheet metal workers who work for contractors may be promoted to positions as supervisors and eventually job superintendents. Those who develop their skills with further training may move into related fields, such as welding. Some sheet metal workers become specialists in particular activities, such as design and layout work or estimating costs of installations. Some workers eventually go into business for themselves as independent sheet metal contractors.

Employment Outlook

Over the next ten to fifteen years, employment in this field is expected to grow at about the same rate as the average for other occupations. The growth in employment will be related to several factors. Many new residential, commercial, and industrial buildings will be constructed, requiring the skills of sheet metal workers, and many older buildings will need to have new energy-efficient heating, cooling, and ventilating systems installed in place of outdated systems. Existing equipment will always need routine maintenance and repair. Decorative sheet metal products are becoming more popular for some uses, a trend that is expected to provide an increasing amount of employment for sheet metal workers. Still, most of the demand for new workers in this field will be to replace experienced people who are transferring to other jobs or leaving the workforce altogether.

Job prospects will vary somewhat with economic conditions. In general, the economy is closely tied to the level of new building construction activity. During economic downturns, workers may face periods of unemployment, while at other times, there may be more jobs than skilled workers available to take them. But overall, sheet metal workers are less affected by economic ups and downs than some other craft workers in the construction field. This is because activities related to maintenance, repair, and replacement of old equipment make up a significant part of their job, and even during an economic slump, building owners are often inclined to go ahead with such work.

Earnings

The median annual earnings for all sheet metal workers in the United States is roughly $39,000. Earnings vary in different parts of the country and tend to be highest in industrialized urban areas. Apprentices begin at about 40 percent of the rate paid to experienced workers and receive periodic pay increases throughout their training. Some workers who are union members are eligible for supplemental pay from their union during periods of unemployment or when they are working less than full time. Many sheet metal workers are members of the Sheet Metal Workers' International Association.

Conditions of Work

Most sheet metal workers have a regular forty-hour workweek and receive extra pay for overtime. Most of their work is performed indoors, so they are less likely to lose time to bad weather than many other craft workers involved in construction projects. Some work is done outdoors, occasionally in uncomfortably hot or cold conditions.

Workers sometimes have to work high above the ground, as when they install gutters and roofs, and sometimes in awkward, cramped positions, as when they install ventilation systems in buildings. Workers may have to be on their feet for long periods, and they may have to lift heavy objects. Possible hazards of the trade include cuts and burns from machinery and equipment, as well as falls from ladders and scaffolding. Workers must use good safety practices to avoid injuries and sometimes wear protective gear such as safety glasses. Sheet metal fabrication shops are usually well ventilated and properly heated and lighted, but at times they are quite noisy.

Sources of Additional Information

■ **National Training Fund for the Sheet Metal and Air Conditioning Industry**
Edward F. Carlough Plaza
601 North Fairfax Street, Suite 240
Alexandria, VA 22314
Tel: 703-739-7200

■ **Sheet Metal and Air Conditioning Contractors' National Association**
PO Box 221230
Chantilly, VA 22022
Tel: 703-803-2980

■ **Sheet Metal Workers' International Association**
1750 New York Avenue, NW
Washington, DC 20006
Tel: 202-783-5880

Stationary Engineers

School Subjects
Mathematics
Physics

Personal Interests
Figuring out how things work
Fixing things

Work Environment
Primarily indoors
Primarily one location

Minimum Education Level
High school diploma
Apprenticeship

Salary Range
$15,600 to $48,000

Certification or Licensing
Required

Outlook
Little change or more slowly than average

DOT: 950   **GOE:** 05.06.02   **NOC:** 7351

Definition

Stationary engineers operate and maintain boilers, engines, air compressors, generators, and other equipment used in providing utilities such as heat, ventilation, light, and power for large buildings, industrial plants, and other facilities. They are called stationary engineers because the equipment they work with is similar to equipment on ships or locomotives, except that it is stationary rather than on a moving vehicle.

History

During the Industrial Revolution of the eighteenth and nineteenth centuries, many new inventions changed the way people lived and worked. Some of these inventions involved the development of new energy sources, including steam engines, coal, electricity, and petroleum. Others were new machines that reduced the need for human labor and increased the efficiency of manufacturing processes. Especially with the application of power to the new machines, many aspects of life began to alter dramatically. A new way of organizing manufacturing arose, the factory system, which relied on dividing manufacturing processes into different functions to be carried out in sequence by many workers. As both the machines and the production processes were refined and improved, the output of industry greatly increased and the lives of ordinary people were transformed by many new products and services.

Among the large machines in factories was equipment that supplied power for the machines used in production. In time, other equipment also supplied heating, cooling, and ventilating for industrial plants. Similar equipment was also used in other large facilities that needed their own utility systems, such as college campuses, department stores, hospitals, military bases, sewage and water treatment plants, and mining operations. Wherever big equipment installations were located, workers were needed to operate and maintain the equipment. Today, the workers responsible for these activities are stationary engineers. They start up, regulate, and shut down the utilities equipment for buildings and building complexes.

Nature of the Work

Stationary engineers are primarily concerned with the safe, efficient, economical operation of utilities equipment. To do their job, they must monitor meters, gauges, and other instruments attached to the equipment. They take regular readings of the instruments and keep a log of information about the operation of the equipment, such as the amount of power produced; the amount of fuel consumed; the composition of gases given off in burning fuel; the temperature, pressure, and water levels inside equipment; and the temperature and humidity of air that has been processed through air-conditioning equipment. When the instrument readings show that the equipment is not operating in the proper ranges, they may control the operation of the equipment with levers, throttles, switches, and valves. They may override automatic controls on the equipment, switch to backup systems, or shut the equipment down.

Periodically, stationary engineers inspect the equipment, looking for any parts that need adjustment, lubrication, or repair. They may tighten loose fittings, replace gaskets and filters, repack bearings, clean burners, oil moving parts, and perform similar maintenance tasks. They may test the water in boilers and add chemicals to the water to prevent scale from building up and clogging water lines. They keep records of all their routine service and repair activities.

Stationary engineers try to prevent breakdowns before they occur. But if unexpected trouble develops in the system, they must identify and correct the problem as soon as possible. They may need only to make minor repairs, or they may have to completely overhaul the equipment, using a variety of hand and power tools.

In large plants, stationary engineers may be responsible for keeping several complex systems in operation. They may be assisted by other workers, such as boiler tenders, air conditioning and refrigeration operators and mechanics, turbine operators, and assistant stationary engineers. In small buildings, just one stationary engineer at a time may be in charge of operating and maintaining the equipment.

Often the instruments and equipment that stationary engineers work with are computer controlled. This means that stationary engineers can keep track of operations throughout a system by reading computer outputs at one central location, rather than checking each piece of equipment. Sensors connected to the computers may monitor factors such as temperature and humidity in the building, and the information they gather can be processed to help stationary engineers make decisions about operating the equipment.

Requirements

Stationary engineers may learn the skills they need by completing apprenticeships, or they may learn through informal on-the-job training, often in combination with course work at a vocational or technical school. A high school diploma or its equivalent is a requirement for either kind of training, and some college may be an advantage. Mechanical aptitude, manual dexterity, and good physical condition are also important. Because of the similarities between marine and stationary power plants, training in marine engineering during service in the U.S. Navy or Merchant Marine can be an excellent background for people who plan on going into this field. However, even after such experience, further training and study are necessary to become a stationary engineer.

Apprenticeships combine a planned program of on-the-job training with classroom instruction in related fields. Apprenticeships are administered by local committees representing both the management of companies that employ stationary engineers and the union to which many stationary engineers belong, the International Union of Operating Engineers. While local committees may establish slightly different requirements, they generally prefer applicants for apprenticeships who have taken courses in computers, mathematics, physics, chemistry, mechanical drawing, and machine shop.

Apprenticeships usually last four years. In the practical experience part of their training, apprentices learn how to operate, maintain, and repair stationary equipment such as blowers, generators, compressors, motors, and refrigeration machinery. They become familiar with precision measurement devices such as calipers and micrometers; hand and machine tools, including electric grinders, lathes, and drill presses; and hoists, blocks, and other equipment used in lifting heavy machines. In the classroom, apprentices study technical subjects that they can use in their work, such as practical chemistry and physics, applied mathematics, computers, blueprint reading, electricity and electronics, and instrumentation.

People who learn their skills on the job work under the supervision of experienced stationary engineers. They may start as boiler tenders or helpers, doing simple tasks that require no special skills, and learn gradually through practical experience. If their job offers few opportunities to learn new skills, it may take many years for workers to acquire all the skills they need. The process may go more quickly if they take courses at a vocational or technical school in subjects such as computerized controls and instrumentation.

Even after they are well trained and experienced in their field, stationary engineers should take short courses to update their knowledge of the equipment they work with. Employers often pay for this kind of additional training. When new equipment is installed in a building, representatives of the equipment manufacturer may present special training programs to introduce its functions.

Most states and cities require that stationary engineers be licensed to operate equipment. There are several classes of license, depending on the kind of equipment and its steam pressure or horsepower. A first-class license qualifies workers to operate any equipment, regardless of size or capacity. Stationary engineers in charge of large equipment complexes and those who supervise other workers need this kind of license. Other classes of licenses limit the capacities or types of equipment that the license holders may operate without supervision.

The requirements for obtaining these licenses vary from place to place. In general, applicants must meet certain training and experience requirements for the class of license, pass a written examination, and be at least eighteen years old and a resident of the city or state for a specified period of time. When licensed stationary engineers move to another city or state, they may have to meet different licensure requirements and take a different examination.

Opportunities for Experience & Exploration

A good way of to find out about this work is to get a part-time or summer job in an industrial plant or another large facility where utility equipment is run by a stationary engineer. Even an unskilled position, such as custodian in a boiler room, can provide an opportunity to observe the work and working conditions in this occupation. A talk with a stationary engineer or a union representative may also prove helpful.

Methods of Entering

Stationary engineers often start out working as craft workers in other fields. Information about job openings, apprenticeships, and other training for this field may be obtained through the local offices of the state employment service or the International Union of Operating Engineers. State and city licensing agencies can give details on local licensure requirements and perhaps possible job leads as well.

Advancement

Experienced stationary engineers may advance to jobs in which they are responsible for operating and maintaining larger or more complex equipment installations. Such job changes may become possible as stationary engineers obtain higher classes of licenses. But obtaining these licenses does not guarantee advancement. Many first-class stationary engineers must work as assistants to other first-class stationary engineers until a position becomes available. Stationary engineers may also move into positions as boiler inspectors, chief plant engineers, building superintendents, building managers, or technical instructors. Additional training or formal education may be needed for some of these positions.

Employment Outlook

Over the next ten to fifteen years, the total number of people employed in this field is expected to change little. Although industrial and commercial development will continue, and thus more equipment will be installed and need to be operated by stationary engineers, much of the new equipment will be automated and computerized. The greater efficiency of such controls and instrumentation will tend to reduce the demand for stationary engineers. Nonetheless, many job openings will develop in this field when workers transfer to other jobs or leave the workforce altogether. Opportunities will be best for workers who have completed apprenticeships or technical school training.

Earnings

Earnings of stationary engineers vary widely, usually falling between $15,600 and $48,000 a year. The median annual salary is $31,400. In metropolitan areas, where most jobs are located, earnings tend to be higher than in nonmetropolitan areas. Stationary engineers in metropolitan areas of the West have the highest average earnings, those in the South have the lowest, with workers in the Midwest and Northeast closer to the national average for metropolitan areas.

Most stationary engineers receive fringe benefits in addition to their regular wages. Benefits may include life and health insurance, paid vacation and sick days, employer reimbursement for work-related courses, and pension plans.

Conditions of Work

Stationary engineers usually work shifts of about eight hours, five days a week. Because the plants where they work may operate twenty-four hours a day, some stationary engineers regularly work afternoon or night shifts, weekends, or holidays. Some work rotating shifts. Occasionally overtime hours are necessary, such as when equipment breaks down and must be returned to functioning as soon as possible.

Most boiler rooms, power plants, and engine rooms are clean and well lighted, but stationary engineers may still encounter some uncomfortable conditions in the course of their work. They may be exposed to high temperatures, dirt, grease, odors, and smoke. At times they may need to crouch, kneel, crawl inside equipment, or work in awkward positions. They may spend much of their time on their feet. There is some danger attached to working around boilers and electrical and mechanical equipment, but following good safety practices greatly reduces the possibility of injury. By staying constantly on the alert, stationary engineers can avoid burns, electrical shock, and injuries from moving parts.

Sources of Additional Information

■ **International Union of Operating Engineers**
1125 17th Street, NW
Washington, DC 20036
Tel: 202-429-9100

■ **National Association of Power Engineers, Inc.**
5-7 Springfield Street
Chicopee, MA 01013
Tel: 413-592-6273

Surveying and Mapping Technicians

School Subjects
Geography
Mathematics

Personal Interests
Computers
Drawing/painting

Work Environment
Primarily outdoors
Primarily multiple locations

Minimum Education Level
High school diploma

Salary Range
$13,400 to $43,700

Certification or Licensing
Voluntary

Outlook
More slowly than the average

DOT: 018   **GOE:** 05.01.06   **NOC:** 2254

Definition

Surveying and mapping technicians help determine, describe, and record geographic areas or features. They are usually the leading helper to the professional surveyor, civil engineer, and mapmaker. In their work they use modern surveying and mapping instruments and need to understand the scientific principles and mathematics behind each method of measurement and recording. They are prepared to participate in photogrammetric surveying and mapping operations. Surveying and mapping technicians also have a basic knowledge of the current practices and legal implications of surveys to establish and record property size, shape, topography, and boundaries. They often supervise assistants during routine surveying conducted within bounds established by a professional surveyor.

History

From ancient times, people have needed to define their property boundaries. Marking established areas of individual or group ownership was a basis for the development of early civilizations. Landholding became important in ancient Egypt, and with the development of hieroglyphics people were able to keep a record of their holdings. Eventually, nations found it necessary not only to mark property boundaries but also to lay out and record principal routes of commerce and transportation. For example, records of the Babylonians tell of their canals and irrigation ditches. The Romans surveyed and mapped their empire's principal roads.

The surveying process using instruments traditionally required at least two people. A scientist who had mastered the technology of the times was the leader, or professional surveyor. Helpers made measurements with chains, tapes, and wheel rotations, where each rotation accounted for a known length of distance. The helpers held rods with measured marks for location and drove stakes or placed other markers to define important points. As the measuring instruments became more complex, the speed, scope, and accuracy of the surveying process increased. As a result, the surveyor's assistants needed to know more about the equipment and the process to be able to work on the surveying team. For most modern surveying operations of any size, a surveying technician is the leading helper to the professional surveyor. Therefore, the technician's tasks are usually closely associated with those of the professional surveyor.

As the United States expanded, surveyors and their technical helpers were among the first and most needed workers: they established new land ownership by surveying and filing claims. Since then, precise and accurate geographical measurements have always been needed, whether to determine the location of a highway; the site of a building; the right-of-way for drainage ditches, telephone, or power lines; or for the charting of unexplored land, bodies of water, or underground mines. Through the years, the science of measurement has improved our ability to establish exact locations and determine distances. In these processes, most of the actual measuring work is done by surveying technicians and other helpers under the direction of professional surveyors.

Developments in surveying and mapping technology have made great changes in the planning and construction of highway systems and in the design and building of stationary structures of all kinds. In surveying for roadway route selection and design, technicians increasingly use photogrammetry, which uses automatic plotting machines to scribe routes from aerial photographs of rural or urban areas. Route data obtained by photogrammetry may then be processed through computers to calculate land acquisition, grading, and construction costs. Photogrammetry is faster and far more accurate than former methods. New electronic distance-measuring devices have brought surveying to a higher level of technology. Technicians can measure distance more quickly, accurately, and economically than possible with tapes or rod and chain. This requires better educated technicians to serve as chief assistants in complex surveying operations.

The new technological advances and the use of computers in data processing have made surveying and mapping technical careers more complex and challenging than just a few decades ago. These changes have further increased surveying and mapping's accuracy, and extended its use to include making detailed maps of ocean floors and the moon. Surveying and mapping technicians must be able to use specialized techniques as they assist surveyors or scientists in charge of surveys. For example, every missile fired from the Kennedy Space Center is tracked electronically to determine if it is on course. Mapmakers have recently used photogrammetry to map the moon. The technological complexity of such undertakings allows professional surveyors to delegate more tasks to technicians than ever before.

Nature of the Work

As essential assistants to civil engineers, surveyors, and mapmakers, surveying and mapping technicians are usually the first to be involved in any job that requires precise plotting. This includes highways, airports, housing developments, mines, dams, bridges, and buildings of all kinds.

The surveying and mapping technician is a key worker in field parties or major surveying projects and is often assigned the position of *chief instrument worker* under the surveyor's supervision. In this capacity, technicians use a variety of surveying instruments including the theodolite, transit, level, and different types of electronic equipment to measure distance or locate a position. As a transit worker, the technician uses many of these instruments—assembling, adjusting, sighting, and reading them. A *rod worker,* using a level rod or range pole, helps make elevation and distance measurements. A *chain worker* measures shorter distances and uses the surveyor's chain or a metal tape. In the course of a survey, it is important to accurately record all readings and keep orderly field notes so that the survey can be checked for accuracy.

Surveying and mapping technicians may specialize if they join a surveying firm that focuses on one or more particular types of surveying. In a firm that specializes in land surveying, technicians are highly skilled in technical measuring and tasks related to establishing township, property, and other tract-of-land boundary lines. They help the professional surveyor with maps, notes, or actual land title deeds. They help survey the land, check the accuracy of existing records, and prepare legal documents such as deeds and leases.

Similarly, technicians who work for highway, pipeline, railway, or power line surveying firms help to establish points, grades, lines, and other points of reference for construction projects. This survey information provides the exact locations for engineering design and construction work.

Technicians who work for a geodetic surveyor help take measurements of large masses of land, sea, or space. These measurements must take into account the curvature of the earth and its geophysical characteristics. This information sets major points of reference for smaller land surveys, determining national boundaries and preparing maps.

Technicians also specialize in measurements for hydrographic surveyors. Hydrographic surveyors make surveys of harbors, rivers, and other bodies of water. These surveys are needed to design navigation systems; plan and build breakwaters, levees, dams, locks, piers, and bridges; prepare nautical maps and charts; and establish property boundaries. Technicians are key workers in making these surveys; they often supervise other workers as they make measurements and record data.

In mining companies, the technician is usually a member of the engineering, scientific, or management team. Working from the survey or engineering office, technicians take part in regular mine surveying. They set up the instructions and limits of the work team. In the office, technicians make survey calculations, develop maps, and calculate the tonnage of ore and broken rock.

In recent years, costly new surveying instruments have changed the way mining survey technicians do their jobs. These technicians work on the geological staffs of either mining companies or exploration companies. At operating mines, technicians may map underground geology; sample, locate diamond drill holes, log drill cores, and map geological data derived from boreholes. They may map data on mine plans and diagrams and help the geologist determine ore reserves.

In the search for new mines, *mining survey technicians* operate delicate instruments to obtain data on variations in the earth's magnetic field, its conductivity, or gravity. They use the data to map the boundaries of potential areas for further exploration.

Surveying and mapping technicians may find topographical surveys to be interesting and challenging work. These determine the contours of the land and indicate such features as mountains, lakes, rivers, forests, roads, farms, buildings, and other distinguishable landmarks.

In topographical surveying, technicians often help take aerial or land photographs with special equipment installed in an airplane or ground station that permits pictures of large areas to be made. This is called photogrammetry. From these pictures, accurate measurements of the terrain and of surface features can be made. These surveys are helpful in highway planning and in the preparation of topographical maps. Photogrammetry is particularly helpful in charting areas that are inaccessible or difficult to travel. The method is widely used to measure farm land planted with certain crops and to verify crop average allotments under government production planning quotas.

By far the largest number of survey technicians are employed in construction work. Technicians are needed from start to finish on any construction job. They keep the structure's progress within engineering specifications for size, height, depth, level, and geometric form. Surveying technicians locate the critical construction points on the job site as specified on design plans within the bounds of the property. They locate corners of buildings, foundation detail points, center points for columns, walls, and other features, height of floor or ceiling levels, and other points that require precise measurements and location.

Several entry-level technician positions available in the fields of drafting, mapping, geodetic surveying, and geological exploration are described in the following paragraphs.

Survey helpers, surveyors, or *survey drafters* operate surveying instruments to gather numerical data. They calculate tonnage broken and incentive pay, map mine development, and provide precise directions and locations to the workforce. Under direction, they conduct studies on operations and equipment to improve methods and to reduce costs.

Assistant field or exploration geologists operate a variety of geophysical instruments on a grid pattern to obtain data on variations in the earth's magnetism, conductivity, and gravity. They map the data and analyze stream waters, soils, and rocks from known locations to search for ore occurrences. Such technicians often work in remote areas.

Highway technicians, under the direction of a surveyor, make surveys and estimate costs. They also help plan, lay out, and supervise the construction and maintenance of highways. *Party chiefs* for licensed land surveyors survey land for boundary line locations and plan subdivisions and additions to cities.

Photogrammetric technicians use aerial photographs to prepare maps, mosaics, plans, and profiles.

Rail or waterway surveying technicians make surveys, specifications, and cost estimates to help plan and construct railway or waterway facilities.

Topographical drafters or *photocartographers* draw and correct topographical maps from source data such as surveying notes, old maps, or photographs. They may be part of a surveying crew in the field to compile original measurement data.

Requirements

A high school diploma or its equivalent is a basic requirement for most opportunities in a surveying technician career.

Future surveying and mapping technicians should take all the mathematics, science, and communications courses available in high school. They should also take other courses that are part of the school's general college-preparatory program. Mathematics courses should include at least two years of algebra, and plane and solid geometry and trigonometry, as well as mechanical drawing. Physics, including laboratory experience, as well as chemistry and biology are also valuable.

Nearly all mapping is now computerized, so surveying and mapping technicians need strong computer skills. High school students should take as many computer courses as possible.

Reading, writing, and comprehension skills are vital in surveying and mapping. Four years of high school English and language skills courses are highly recommended. Reports and letters are an essential part of the technician's work, so a firm grasp of English, grammar, and spelling is important.

It is sometimes possible to enter the field of surveying immediately after high school by securing a position where on-the-job training is provided. To advance, the prospective technician can expect to supplement the job experience by taking courses in surveying. However, this method of becoming a technician can take a long time. It involves several years of intensive part-time formal study to master the basic science and technical knowledge of the field.

Graduates of accredited post-high school training programs who have a strong background in surveying, photogrammetry, and mapping are in the best position to enter the field as beginning surveying and mapping technicians. Opportunities for this kind of training are available in postsecondary programs at junior colleges, technical institutes, and specialized schools. These are demanding technical programs, usually two academic years long and sometimes with field study in the summer. Typical courses in the first year include English, composition, drafting, applied mathematics, surveying and measurements, construction materials and methods, applied physics, statistics, and computer applications.

The second year courses continue with technical physics, advanced surveying, photogrammetry and mapping, soils and foundations, technical reporting, legal practices and problems, industrial organizations and institutions, and transportation and environmental engineering.

Such a program can form a base for employment; later, with additional part-time study, the technician can specialize in geodesy, topography, hydrography, or photogrammetry. Many graduates of two-year programs later pursue a bachelor's degree in surveying, engineering, or geomatics.

Because surveying and mapping technicians may spend considerable time in field surveys, candidates should have an interest in working outdoors. Technicians must work with other people and often direct or supervise them. They must, therefore, have strong leadership qualities.

The ability to work easily with numbers and to perform mathematical computations accurately and quickly is very important in a surveying and mapping career. Equally important is the ability to understand and effectively use words and ideas. Those who can visualize objects in two or three dimensions and can discriminate among and compare shapes, sizes, lines, shadings, and other aspects of objects and pictures of objects will be at a distinct advantage over their peers.

To function as members of a survey party in the field, technicians are usually required to be in good physical condition and must be able to negotiate all types of terrain. Surveying technicians are on their feet a great deal of the time. Often they must carry the surveying instruments and equipment.

Surveying and mapping technicians need excellent eyesight to read precision optical instruments used in modern surveying. Their hearing must be good because members of surveying teams sometimes have to shout over distances. However, radio communication is now becoming the common way to communicate. In either case, the surveying and mapping technician must give instructions clearly and precisely. Endurance and coordination are important physical assets for the surveying technician.

Unlike professional land surveyors, there are no special requirements for registration or licensing for surveying and mapping technicians. However, technicians who seek government employment must pass a civil service examination.

To advance their professional standing and become more attractive to a wider variety of employers, surveying and mapping technicians should try to become certified engineering technicians. This certification is similar to the licensing of engineers, but the requirements are based on and consistent with the tasks, skills, and responsibilities that are expected of these technicians.

Surveying and mapping technicians may also, upon completion of the required years of service, take an examination for licensing as a licensed land surveyor. Successful completion of this examination enables these enterprising technicians to operate their own surveying businesses.

Opportunities for Experience & Exploration

One of the best opportunities for experience is a summer job with a construction firm or a company involved in survey work. Even if the job does not involve direct contact with survey crews, it will provide an opportunity to observe them at work and discover more about their activities.

Methods of Entering

A few high school graduates without formal surveying training are hired as rod workers or chain workers with a surveying firm and may eventually become qualified technicians by combining experience with part-time coursework.

Graduates of a technical institute or a four-year college will find their school's placement service helpful in arranging examinations or interviews. Regular employers of surveying technicians often send recruiters to schools before graduation and arrange to employ promising graduates. In many cities, there are employment agencies that specialize in placing technical workers in positions in surveying, mapping, construction, mining, and related fields.

Graduates of junior college and technical institute programs can enter the field immediately as instrument workers. Later, they can become surveyor aides, instrument operators, computers, observers, recorders, or plane-table operators.

Some community or technical colleges have work-study programs that provide cooperative part-time or summer work for pay. Employers involved with these programs will hire students full time after graduation.

Advancement

Possibilities for advancement are linked to the level of the technician's formal education and experience. As they gain experience and technical knowledge, technicians can advance to positions of greater responsibility and eventually to surveyor or chief of a surveying party. The latter, however, is almost impossible without formal education beyond high school.

Steps are being taken by some of the professional engineering and surveying associations to increase the requirements needed to become a registered or licensed land surveyor. One requirement being considered is a bachelor's degree in engineering. If this action is taken, it will be nearly impossible for the high school graduate to advance to higher levels or professional positions. Accordingly, advancement will be more difficult for the technicians who graduated from formal two-year technical programs in surveying technology. Graduates of two- and three-year programs can usually transfer at least a part of their college-level credits to degree-granting engineering programs if they decide they want to obtain a professional degree and become a registered professional surveyor. Some survey workers choose to work for a year or two before continuing with their formal education. Others make the transfer immediately upon completion of their two- or three-year degree program.

The surveying technician must continue studying to keep up with the technological developments in surveying, measuring, and mapping. Computers, lasers, and microcomputers will continue to change the job requirements. Studying to keep up with changes, combined with experience gained on the job, increases the technician's value to his or her employers.

Employment Outlook

The employment outlook in the surveying and mapping field is expected to be good through the year 2005, although the projected growth is more slowly than the average. This outlook applies to those students who have attained at least two years of junior college or technical institute preparation as surveying or civil engineering technicians.

One of the factors that is expected to increase the demand for surveying services—and therefore surveying technicians—is growth in urban and suburban areas. New streets, homes, shopping centers, schools, and gas and water lines will require property and boundary-line surveys.

Other factors are the continuing state and federal highway improvement programs and the increasing number of urban redevelopment programs. The expansion of industrial and business firms and the relocation of some firms in large undeveloped tracts are also expected to create a need for surveying services.

The continuing search for new petroleum fields and mineral deposits involves increasingly complex measurements and surveying techniques. Exploring for oil and gas will require the services of many technicians on surveying teams.

Although new electronic equipment reduces the time necessary to complete land surveys, it is not expected to decrease the number of job opportunities. The new equipment and technology introduced into the surveying field will continue to require additional educational preparation at the technician or instrument worker level.

Earnings

Most surveying and mapping technicians earn between $17,400 and $40,000 a year, and the average is around $28,000 a year. Some technicians, especially those at the very beginning of their careers, may earn as little as $13,400 a year, while some senior technicians with special skills and experience may earn as much as $43,700 a year or more.

In the mid-1990s, surveying and mapping technicians with two-year degrees working for the federal government receive starting salaries of around $16,000 a year, and the overall average salary for surveying technicians working for the government is around $25,000 a year.

Conditions of Work

Surveying and mapping technicians usually work about forty hours a week except when overtime is necessary. The peak work period for many kinds of surveying work is during the summer months when weather conditions are most favorable. However, it is not uncommon for surveying crews to be exposed to all types of weather conditions. Surveying technicians on construction jobs who, with their helpers, take daily point-to-point and step-by-step measurements on construction jobs must work in all kinds of weather.

Some survey projects involve certain hazards depending upon the region and the climate as well as local plant and animal life. Field survey crews encounter snakes and poison ivy. They are subject to heat exhaustion, sunburn, and frostbite. Some survey projects, particularly those being conducted near construction projects or busy highways, impose the dangers of injury from cars and flying debris. Unless survey technicians are employed for office assignments, where working conditions are similar to those of other office workers, their work location quite likely will change from survey to survey. Some assignments may require technicians to be away from home for varying periods of time.

While on the job, surveying crews and especially technicians who often supervise other workers must take special care to observe good safety practices. Construction and mining workplaces are usually "hard-hat" areas where special clothing and protective hats and shoes are required.

Surveying and mapping technicians must be patient, orderly, systematic, accurate, and objective in their work. They must be able to work in a subordinate role as an assistant to the surveyor or cartographer. They must be willing to work cooperatively and have the ability to think and plan ahead. One of the most important qualities is a willingness to work long hours for extended periods, as is sometimes required in the work of all technicians.

These technicians' careers offer great potential for job satisfaction. Well-prepared and experienced technicians can secure positions that require extensive travel and exposure to varied conditions of living, from field campsites to hotel accommodations. As the survey party moves from one location to another, these technicians will find that each assignment is unique. Each new assignment represents an opportunity to open new areas to develop. In this sense, the technician becomes a part of an exploration team. In the more routine, and perhaps less adventuresome tasks, the surveying technician performs an essential and especially valuable social and commercial service.

Sources of Additional Information

■ **Accreditation Board for Engineering and Technology**
111 Market Place
Baltimore, MD 21202
Tel: 410-347-7700

■ **American Congress on Surveying and Mapping**
5410 Grosvenor Lane, Suite 100
Bethesda, MD 20814
Tel: 301-493-0200
WWW: http://www.acsm-hqtrs.org/acsm/

■ **American Institute of Mining, Metallurgical, and Petroleum Engineers**
345 East 47th Street, 14th Floor
New York, NY 10017
Tel: 212-705-7695

■ **American Society for Photogrammetry and Remote Sensing**
5410 Grosvenor Lane, Suite 210
Bethesda, MD 20814
Tel: 301-493-0290

Surveyors

School Subjects
Geography
Mathematics

Personal Interests
Computers
Drawing/painting

Work Environment
Primarily outdoors
Primarily multiple locations

Minimum Education Level
Bachelor's degree

Salary Range
$13,400 to $47,600

Certification or Licensing
Required

Outlook
More slowly than the average

DOT: 018   **GOE:** 05.01.06   **NOC:** 2154

Definition

Surveyors mark exact measurements and locations of elevations, points, lines, and contours on or near the earth's surface. They measure the distances between points to determine property boundaries and to provide data for mapmaking, construction projects, and other engineering purposes.

History

As the United States expanded from the Atlantic to the Pacific, people moved over the mountains and plains into the uncharted regions of the West. They found it necessary to mark their routes and to mark property lines and borderlines by surveying and filing claims. The need for precise and accurate geographical measurements and precise records of those measurements has increased over the years: for the location of a trail, highway, or road; the site of a log cabin, frame house, or skyscraper; the right-of-way for water pipes, drainage ditches, or telephone lines; or for the charting of unexplored regions, bodies of water, land, or underground mines. As we improved our ability to establish exact locations and to measure points on the surface of the earth, from the deepest point in the ocean to mountain tops, it has become the work of the professional surveyor.

Nature of the Work

The surveyor's *party chief* and party are usually the first workers to be involved in any job requiring the precise determination of points, locations, lines, or elevations. On proposed construction projects—superhighways, airstrips, housing developments, bridges—it is the surveyor's responsibility to make the necessary measurements by conducting an accurate and detailed survey of the area.

The surveyor usually works with a field party consisting of several people. *Instrument assistants* handle a variety of surveying instruments including the theodolite, transit, level, surveyor's chain, rod, and different types of electronic equipment used to measure distance or locate a position. In the course of the survey, it is important that all readings be accurately recorded and that field notes be maintained so that the survey can be checked for accuracy by the surveyor.

Surveyors may become expert in one or more particular types of surveying. *Land surveyors* establish township, property, and other tract-of-land boundary lines. Using maps, notes, or actual land title deeds, they survey the land, checking the accuracy of existing records. This information is used to prepare legal documents such as deeds and leases. *Land surveying managers* coordinate the work of land surveyors and their survey parties with that of legal, engineering, architectural, and other staff involved with the project. In addition, these managers develop policies, prepare budgets, certify work upon completion, and handle numerous other administrative duties.

A *highway surveyor* establishes points, grades, lines, and other points of reference for highway construction projects. This survey information is essential to the work of the numerous engineers and the construction crews who will actually plan and build the new highway.

A *geodetic surveyor* measures such large masses of land, sea, or space that the measurements must take into account the curvature of the earth and its geophysical characteristics. This person's work is helpful in establishing points of reference for smaller land surveys, for determining national boundaries, and in preparing maps. *Geodetic computers* calculate latitude, longitude, angles, areas, and other information needed for mapmaking. They work from field notes made by an engineering survey party using reference tables and a calculating machine or computer.

A *marine surveyor* makes surveys of harbors, rivers, and other bodies of water. This person determines the depth of the water, usually by taking soundings or sound measurements, in relation to land masses. These surveys are essential in planning navigation projects; in developing plans for and constructing breakwaters, dams, piers, marinas, and bridges; or in constructing nautical charts and maps.

A *mine surveyor* makes surface and underground surveys, preparing maps of mines and mining operations. Such maps are helpful in examining underground passages on and between levels and in assessing the strata and volume of raw material available.

A *geophysical prospecting surveyor* locates and marks sites considered likely to contain petroleum deposits. *Oil-well directional surveyors* use sonic, electronic, or nuclear measuring instruments to gauge the characteristics of earth formations in boreholes from which they evaluate the productivity of oil- or gas-bearing reservoirs. A *pipeline surveyor* determines rights-of-way for oil pipeline construction projects. This surveyor establishes the right-of-way and property lines and assembles the information essential to the preparation for and laying of the lines.

A *photogrammetric engineer* determines the contour of an area to show elevations and depressions and indicates such features as mountains, lakes, rivers, forests, roads, farms, buildings, and other landmarks. Aerial, land, or water photographs used in their work are taken with special photographic equipment installed in the airplane or ground station that permits pictures of large areas to be made. From these pictures accurate measurements of the terrain and of surface features can be made. These surveys are helpful in highway and engineering planning and in the preparation of topographical maps. Photogrammetry, as photo surveying is termed, is particularly helpful in charting areas that are inaccessible or difficult to travel.

Requirements

High school students interested in a career as a surveyor should take algebra, geometry, and trigonometry, physics, mechanical drawing, and other related science or drafting courses.

After high school, students should take a four-year college program in surveying or engineering. Civil engineering, with a surveying emphasis, is a common major selected by students wishing to become surveyors because the two fields are so closely allied. Graduate study is necessary for advancement in the highly technical areas.

Because the surveyor spends a great deal of time in field surveys, an interest in working outdoors is necessary. Surveying involves working with other people and often requires directing or supervising the work of others. Therefore, a surveyor must have leadership qualities for supervisory positions.

The ability to work with numbers and to perform mathematical computations accurately and quickly is very important. Other abilities that are helpful in surveying work include the ability to visualize and understand objects in two or three dimensions (spatial relationships) and the ability to discriminate between and compare shapes, sizes, lines, shadings, and other forms (form perception). Surveyors do a great deal of walking. They may also have to carry equipment over all types of terrain. Endurance, coordination, and the ability to compensate for physical impairment are important physical assets for the surveyor.

All fifty states require that surveyors making property and boundary surveys be licensed or registered. The requirements for licensure vary, but in general they include one of the following: be a college graduate with two to four years of experience; have at least six years' experience and be able to pass an examination in land surveying; or have at least ten years' experience. Information on specific requirements can be obtained by contacting the appropriate state agency in the capital of the state in which one wishes to work. Those who seek employment in the federal government must take a civil service examination and meet the educational, experience, and other specified requirements for the position in which they are interested.

Opportunities for Experience & Exploration

One of the best opportunities for experience is to seek a summer job with a construction outfit or a company that is planning survey work. This may be private or government work. Even if the job does not involve direct contact with survey crews, it will offer an opportunity to observe them at work and to talk informally with them about surveying.

Some colleges have work-study programs that will permit periodic on-the-job experiences. These opportunities, like summer and part-time jobs, can be beneficial to the person who is considering this field as a career.

Methods of Entering

Some people get jobs as instrument assistants with a surveying firm. College graduates will find the placement service of their institution to be very helpful in arranging for necessary examinations or interviews. In many cities there are employment agencies that specialize in positions in surveying and related fields.

Advancement

Surveyors with the highest level of education and initiative in keeping up with technological developments in the field can become party chiefs.

There are many who believe that surveying has been too long isolated from engineering, and that land surveying is engineering. With the increasing requirement of an engineering degree for entrance to surveying in several states, it will be easier to transfer to a larger number of related positions. Although a surveying or civil engineering program is recommended for a prospective surveyor, one could major in electrical, mechanical, or chemical engineering. Drafting is another related field to which a surveyor might move.

Employment Outlook

In the 1990s, nearly half of the estimated 108,000 surveyors in the United States are employed in engineering, architectural, and surveying firms. Federal, state, and local government agencies employ about one-fourth, and most of the rest work for construction companies, oil and gas extraction companies, and public utilities. Approximately 6,000 surveyors are self-employed.

The employment outlook in surveying through the end of the 1990s is expected to be good, although the U.S. Department of Labor predicts the field will grow more slowly than the average. In view of the pressure for preparation in engineering as a prerequisite for professional status and licensure, opportunities will be better for those who have college degrees.

Some of the factors that are expected to increase the demand for surveyors include: growth in urban and suburban areas, with new streets, homes, shopping centers, schools, gas and water lines requiring property and boundary line surveys; expanding state and federal highway improvement programs; increasing number of urban redevelopment programs; expansion of industrial and business firms and the relocation of some firms in large undeveloped tracts; and increasing demand for land and nautical maps and charts. However, many

176

such projects can be canceled or postponed during times of economic stress; therefore, openings for surveyors depend in part on the state of the national and local economy.

Although new electronic equipment and devices are reducing the time necessary to complete land surveys, it is not expected that they will reduce the number of opportunities available. Instead, the new equipment may create a need for additional training.

Earnings

The median annual earnings for surveyors in the 1990s are about $26,800. The federal government hires high school graduates as surveyor helpers at about $13,400 per year and as instrument assistants at about $15,100 per year. The federal government hires land surveyors at about $17,600 per year, depending on their qualifications. The average salary for all land surveyors in the federal government is $32,800. Highly skilled geodetic surveyors can earn up to $47,600.

In private industry, beginning salaries are comparable to those offered by the federal government, according to the limited information available. Most positions with the federal, state, and local governments and with private firms provide the usual medical, pension, insurance benefits, and vacation and holiday periods.

Conditions of Work

The surveyor works the usual forty-hour week except when overtime is necessary to complete a survey so that a project can be started immediately. The peak work period for the surveyor comes during the summer months when weather conditions are most favorable. However, it is not uncommon for the surveyor to be exposed to all types of weather conditions.

Some survey projects involve a certain amount of hazard, depending upon the region and the climate as well as the plant and animal life. Field survey crews encounter snakes, poison ivy, and other plant and animal life; they are subject to heat exhaustion, sunburn, and frostbite. Some survey projects, particularly those being conducted near construction projects or busy highways, impose the dangers of injury from heavy traffic, flying objects, and other accidental hazards. Much of the surveying of vast lands and large mountain formations is beginning to be done with satellite technology. So remote area studies may become less frequent. However, small areas of study will be more cost-effective when surveyed by teams on the ground. Unless the surveyor is employed for office assignments, where the working conditions are similar to those of other office workers, the work location quite likely will change from survey to survey. Some assignments may necessitate being away from home for varying periods of time.

Sources of Additional Information

■ **American Congress on Surveying and Mapping**
5410 Grosvenor Lane, Suite 100
Bethesda, MD 20814
Tel: 301-493-0200
WWW: http://www.acsm-hqtrs.org/acsm/

■ **American Society for Photogrammetry and Remote Sensing**
5410 Grosvenor Lane, Suite 210
Bethesda, MD 20814
Tel: 301-493-0290

Welders

School Subjects
 Physics
 Shop

Personal Interests
 Building things
 Cars

Work Environment
 Indoors and outdoors
 Primarily multiple locations

Minimum Education Level
 High school diploma
 Apprenticeship

Salary Range
 $16,000 to $45,000+

Certification or Licensing
 Required for certain positions

Outlook
 More slowly than the average

DOT: 810   **GOE:** 05.05.06   **NOC:** 7265

Definition

Welders operate a variety of special equipment to join metal parts together permanently, usually using heat and sometimes pressure. They work on constructing and repairing automobiles, aircraft, ships, buildings, bridges, highways, appliances, and many other metal structures and manufactured products.

History

Although some welding techniques were used more than a thousand years ago in forging iron blades by hand, modern welding processes were first employed beginning in about the 1880s. From experimental beginnings, the pioneers in this field developed a wide variety of innovative processes. These included resistance welding, invented in 1877, in which an electric current is sent through metal parts in contact. Electrical resistance and pressure melt the metal at the area of contact. Gas welding, also developed in the same era, is a relatively simple process using a torch that burns a gas such as acetylene to create enough heat to melt and fuse metal parts. Oxyacetylene welding, a version of this process developed a few years later, is a common welding process today. Arc welding, first used commercially in 1889, relies on an electric arc to generate heat. Thermite welding, which fuses metal pieces with the intense heat of a chemical reaction, was first used about 1900.

In the twentieth century, the sudden demand for vehicles and armament, and a growing list of industrial uses for welding that resulted from the two world wars have spurred researchers to keep improving welding processes and also have encouraged the development of numerous new processes. Today there are more than eighty different types of welding and related processes. Some of the newer processes include laser beam welding and electron beam welding.

Many welding processes have specialized applications. Welders need not be familiar with every kind of welding process and equipment, and in fact many welders use only one process in their work. The kind of welding that welders do depends on the job that needs to be done, their training, and the available equipment.

Nature of the Work

Welders can use various kinds of equipment and processes to create the heat and pressure needed to melt the edges of metal pieces in a controlled fashion, so that the pieces may be joined permanently. The processes can be grouped into three categories. The arc welding process derives heat from an electric arc between two electrodes or between an electrode and the workpiece. The gas welding process produces heat by burning a mixture of oxygen and some other combustible gas, such as acetylene or hydrogen. The resistance welding process obtains heat from pressure and resistance by the workpiece to an electric current. Two of these processes, the arc and gas methods, can also be used to cut, gouge, or finish metal.

Depending on which of these processes and equipment they use, welders may be designated *arc welders, gas welders,* or *acetylene welders; combination welders* (meaning they use a combination of gas and arc welding); or *welding machine operators* (meaning they operate machines that may use either an arc welding process, an electron beam welding process, a laser welding process, or a friction welding process). Other workers in the welding field include *resis-*

tance *machine welders; oxygen cutters,* who use gas torches to cut or trim metals; and *arc cutters,* who use an electric arc to cut or trim metals.

Skilled welders usually begin by planning and laying out their work based on drawings, blueprints, or other specifications. Using their working knowledge of the properties of the metal, they determine the proper sequence of operations needed for the job. They may work with steel, stainless steel, cast iron, bronze, aluminum, nickel, and other metals and alloys. Metal pieces to be welded may be in a variety of positions, such as flat, vertical, horizontal, or overhead.

In the most commonly used of the manual arc welding processes, welders grasp a holder containing a suitable electrode and adjust the electric current supplied to the electrode. Then they strike an arc (create an electric discharge across a gap) by touching the electrode to the metal. Next, they guide the electrode along the metal seam to be welded, allowing sufficient time for the heat of the arc to melt the metal. The molten metal from the electrode is deposited in the joint and, together with the molten metal edges of the base metal, solidifies to form a solid connection. Welders determine the correct kind of electrode to use based on the job specifications and their knowledge of the materials.

In gas welding, welders melt the metal edges with an intensely hot flame from the combustion of fuel gases in welding torches. First they obtain the proper types of torch tips and welding rods, which are rods of a filler metal that goes into the weld seam. They adjust the regulators on the tanks of fuel gases, such as oxygen and acetylene, and light the torch. To obtain the proper size and quality of flame, welders adjust the gas valves on the torch and hold the flame against the metal until it is hot enough. Then they apply the welding rod to the molten metal to supply the extra filler needed to complete the weld.

Maintenance welders, another category of welding workers, may use any of various welding techniques. They travel to construction sites, utility installations, and other locations to make on-site repairs to metalwork.

Some workers in the welding field do repetitive production tasks using automatic welding equipment. In general, automatic welding is not used where there are critical safety and strength requirements. The surfaces that these welders work on are usually in only one position. Resistance machine welders often work in the mass production of parts, doing the same welding operations repeatedly. To operate the welding machine, they first make adjustments to control the electric current and the pressure and then feed in and align the workpieces. After completing the welding operation, welders remove the work from the machine. Welders must constantly monitor the process in order to make sure that the machine is producing the proper weld.

To cut metal, oxygen cutters may use hand-guided torches or machine-mounted torches. They direct the flame of burning oxygen and fuel gas onto the area to be cut until it melts. Then an additional stream of gas is released from the torch, which cuts the metal along previously marked lines. Arc cutters follow a similar procedure in their work, except that they use an electric arc as the source of heat. As in oxygen cutting, an additional stream of gas may be released when cutting the metal.

Requirements

Many welders learn their skills in formal training programs in welding, such as those available in many community colleges, technical institutes, trade schools, and in the armed forces. Some programs are short-term and narrow in focus, while others provide several years of thorough preparation for a variety of good jobs. A high school diploma or its equivalent is required for admission into these programs.

Beginners can also learn welding skills in on-the-job training programs. The length of such training programs ranges from several days or weeks for jobs requiring few skills to a period of one to three years for skilled jobs. Trainees often begin as helpers to experienced workers, doing very simple tasks. As they learn, they are given more challenging work. To learn some skilled jobs, trainees supplement their on-the-job training with formal classroom instruction in technical aspects of the trade.

Various programs sponsored by federal, state, or local governments provide training opportunities in some areas. These training programs, which usually stress the fundamentals of welding, may be in the classroom or on the job and may last from a few weeks to a year. Apprenticeship programs are another possible kind of training. Apprenticeships that teach a range of metalworking skills, including the basics of welding, are run by trade unions such as the International Association of Machinists and Aerospace Workers.

Employers generally prefer to hire applicants who are in good enough physical condition that they can bend, stoop, and work in awkward positions. Applicants also need manual dexterity, good eye-hand coordination, and good eyesight, as well as patience and the ability to concentrate for extended periods as they work on a task. For trainee positions for skilled jobs, high school graduates are preferred, although applicants with at least two years of high school or vocational school may be considered.

Courses that prospective welders should try to include in their high school schedule are mathematics, blueprint reading, mechanical drawing, applied physics, and shop. If possible, the shop courses should cover the basics of welding and working with electricity.

Many people in welding and related occupations belong to unions, including the International Association of Machinists and Aerospace Workers; the International Brotherhood of Boilermakers, Iron Ship Builders, Blacksmiths, Forgers and Helpers; the International Union, United Automobile, Aerospace and Agricultural Implement Workers of America; the United Association of Journeymen and Apprentices of the Plumbing and Pipe Fitting Industry of the United States and Canada; and the United Electrical, Radio, and Machine Workers of America.

To do welding work where the strength of the weld is a critical factor (such as in aircraft, bridges, boilers, or high-pressure pipelines), welders may have to pass employer tests or standardized examinations for certification by government agencies or professional and technical associations.

Opportunities for Experience & Exploration

In many high schools, students can begin to learn welding, related metalworking skills, and the basic principles of working with electricity in shop courses. Courses in drafting, blueprint reading, general science, mathematics, and applied physics and chemistry also introduce concepts that welders need to use in their work.

Perhaps with the help of a teacher or a guidance counselor, students may arrange to visit a workplace where they can observe welders or welding machine operators on the job. Ideally, such a visit can provide a chance to see several welding processes and various kinds of welding work and working conditions, as well as an opportunity to talk with welders about their work.

Methods of Entering

Graduates of good training programs in welding often receive help in finding jobs through their school's placement office. The classified ads section of newspapers usually carries listings of local job openings. Information about openings for trainee positions, apprenticeships, and government training programs, as well as jobs for skilled workers, may be available through the local offices of the state employment service and local offices of unions that organize welding workers. Job seekers can also apply directly to the personnel offices at companies that hire welders.

Advancement

Advancement usually depends on acquiring additional skills. Workers who gain experience and learn new processes and techniques are increasingly valuable to their employers, and they may be promoted to positions as supervisors, inspectors, or welding instructors. With further formal technical training, welders may qualify for welding technician jobs.

Some experienced welders go into business for themselves and open their own welding and repair shops.

Employment Outlook

During the next ten to fifteen years, overall employment in welding and related occupations is expected to change little. Most job openings will develop when experienced workers leave their jobs. However, the outlook varies somewhat by industry. In manufacturing industries, the trend toward increasing automation, including more use of welding robots, is expected to decrease the demand for manual welders and increase the demand for welding machine operators. In construction, wholesale trade, and repair services, more skilled welders will be needed as the economy grows, because the work tends to be less routine in these industries and automation is not likely to be a big factor.

During periods when the economy is in a slowdown, many workers in construction and manufacturing, including some welders, may be laid off.

Earnings

The earnings of welding trades workers vary widely depending on the skills need for the job, the industry, location, and other factors. On average, welders and welding machine operators can expect earnings in the range of $16,000 to $29,000 or more. Highly skilled welders may have earnings ranging from about $26,500 to $45,000, and sometimes much more. In addition to wages, employers often provide fringe benefits, such as health insurance plans, paid vacation time, paid sick time, and pension plans.

Conditions of Work

Workers in welding occupations work in a variety of settings. About two-thirds of welders are employed in manufacturing plants that produce motor vehicles, ships, boilers, machinery, appliances, and other metal products. Most of the remaining welders work for repair shops or construction companies that build bridges, large buildings, pipelines, and similar metal structures. Welding machine operators all work in manufacturing industries. Thus workers may spend their workday inside in well-ventilated and well-lighted shops and factories, outside at a construction site, or in confined spaces, such as in an underground tunnel or inside a large storage tank that is being built.

Welders often encounter hazardous conditions and may need to wear goggles, helmets with protective face plates, protective clothing, safety shoes, and other gear to prevent burns and other injuries. Many metals give off toxic gases and fumes when heated, and workers must be careful to avoid exposure to such harmful substances. Other potential dangers include explosions from mishandling combustible gases and electric shock. Workers in this field must learn the safest ways of carrying out welding work and must always pay attention to safety issues. Various trade and safety organizations have developed rules for welding procedures, safety practices, and health precautions that can reduce the risks of the job to a minimum. Operators of automatic welding machines are exposed to fewer hazards than manual welders and cutters, and they usually need to use less protective gear.

Welding jobs can involve working in uncomfortable positions. Sometimes welders work for short periods in booths that are built to contain sparks and glare. In some jobs, workers must repeat the same process over and over.

Sources of Additional Information

■ **American Welding Society**
550 NW LeJeune Road
Miami, FL 33126
Tel: 305-443-9353

Index

estimators, 6, 13, 21, 34, 42-46, 50, 57, 65, 73, 80, 87, 101, 118, 131, 137, 144
excavation and loading machine operators, 109, 112

field technicians, 167
fillers, 77, 116, 181
finish carpenters, 9-10
finishers, 19-20, 54-59
fitters, 122, 124-126, 135
floor covering installers, 76-82

gas welders, 180
geodetic computers, 174
geodetic surveyors, 164, 173, 177
geological drafters, 50
geologists, 164-165
geophysical drafters, 50
geophysical prospecting survey-or, 174
glass installers, 85
glaziers, 83-89
graders, 109
grips, 78
guards, 56, 88
guidance counselors, 64, 94, 183

heating and refrigeration inspec-tors, 32
heating and ventilating drafters, 49
highway surveyors, 173
highway technicians, 26, 165
hoist and winch operators, 109, 112

inspectors, 6, 28-29, 31-36, 73, 158, 184
instrument assistants, 173, 176-177
ironworker riggers, 93
ironworkers, 90-96

judges, 17, 110

laborers, 5, 19, 37-41, 57, 105, 111, 130-131
land surveying managers, 173
land surveyors, 26-27, 29, 165, 167-168, 173, 177
landscape architects, 49
landscape drafters, 49
lathers, 97-102
licensed land surveyors, 26-27, 29, 165, 167-168

machinists, 64, 97, 182-183
maintenance electricians, 61-63, 66-67
maintenance welders, 181
manufacturers' representatives, 80
mapping technicians, 163, 167
marble setters, 103-107
marine drafters, 49
marine surveyors, 174
markers, 55, 162
mechanical drafters, 49
mechanical inspectors, 32
metal building assemblers, 93
millwrights, 25
mine surveyors, 174
mining survey technicians, 164
mixers, 18, 37, 56, 108-109
models, 24, 33, 50, 64, 76, 83, 147
molding plasterers, 130-131

nozzle cement sprayers, 19

oil and gas drafters, 50
oil-well directional surveyors, 174
operating engineers, 108-113, 156, 158, 160
ornamental ironworkers, 92-94, 96
oxygen cutters, 181-182

paperhangers, 114-120
party chiefs, 26, 165, 173, 176
patent drafters, 49
petroleum engineers, 171